Race Pride and the American Identity

Race Pride and the American Identity

Joseph Tilden Rhea

Harvard University Press / 1997

Cambridge, Massachusetts, and London, England

Library of Congress Cataloging-in-Publication Data
Rhea, Joseph Tilden.
    Race pride and the American identity / Joseph Tilden Rhea.
      p.   cm.
    Includes bibliographical references (p.   ) and index.
    ISBN 0–674–56681–5 (alk. paper)
    1. Minorities—Civil rights—United States—History—20th century.
2. United States—Race relations.   2. United States—Ethnic
relations.   4. Indians of North America—Ethnic identity.   5. Asian
Americans—Ethnic identity.   6. Hispanic Americans—Ethnic identity.
7. Afro-Americans—Ethnic identity.   I. Title.
E184.A1R46   1997
305.8′00973—dc21   97–22046
                                                     CIP

To My Mother and Father

ACKNOWLEDGMENTS

The research for this book was made possible by support from the National Park Service. I appreciate the kindness of Gerard Baker, Kitty Deernose, Gayle Hazelwood, Troy Lissimore, Charles Mayo, David Nathanson, Rosalind Rock, Dean Rowley, Sandy Weber, and Janet Wolf.

Other individuals were generous with their time and insight. My thanks to Robert Benavides, Phil and Edna Bonacich, Randall Collins, Sue Embry, Gary Gabehart, Henry Louis Gates, Jr., John Glenn, Gilberto Hinojosa, Irene Hirano, Stanley Lieberson, Peter Marsden, Bill Michael, Rose Ochi, Mas Okui, Orlando Patterson, Richard Peterson, John Skrentny, Mary Waters, and Christopher Winship.

Working with Harvard University Press was a pleasure. My thanks to Michael Aronson, Anita Safran, and the production staff.

This work developed over years of discussion with Mark Boone and has profited greatly from his careful reading. Errors which remain are my own.

Joseph Tilden Rhea
May 1997 / Boston

CONTENTS

Reserving judgments is a matter of infinite hope.

—F. Scott Fitzgerald, *The Great Gatsby*

Introduction

This work is not about race in American history. It is not about the mistreatment of Indians or the oppression of blacks. Rather, it is about the forces which in the last generation have demanded public recognition of those injustices, and which have changed the national collective memory of the past.

At John F. Kennedy's inauguration in 1961, the poet Robert Frost placed Kennedy's presidency in the context of a long and triumphant history of American achievement:

> Our venture in revolution . . .
> Has justified itself in freedom's story
> Right down to now in glory upon glory.[1]

It was to be a full generation before a President again asked a poet to read at his inauguration. Maya Angelou's recitation for Bill Clinton in 1993 was intended to emphasize the new President's similarity to Kennedy. But her words indicated that in the intervening years both the mood and the memory of the nation had shifted dramatically. Angelou's poem was an extended lament over America's "armed struggles for profit," the "bloody sear" of "cynicism," and the waste of the land. Her description of the American past was so bleak she could find hope only in the future:

> History despite its wrenching pain,
> Cannot be unlived, but if faced
> With courage, need not be lived again.[2]

With such opposing visions of the past, Frost and Angelou naturally arrive at different interpretations of the present and attitudes toward the future. Frost's vision is of a largely Anglo-Saxon country entering a "golden age of poetry and power."[3] In contrast, Angelou's poem names over thirty different American racial and ethnic groups without once using the words America or American. Most of these groups, she reminds us, have suffered great injustice in this country. Thus Angelou warns of the possibility of being "wedded forever to fear, yoked eternally to brutishness."[4]

American consciousness changed dramatically during the years which separate Frost and Angelou, and that change is well reflected in, and partly constituted by, the new public history in this country. The aim of this work is to document the specific reasons why American collective memory has, in the last thirty years, come to better reflect the racial and ethnic diversity of its citizenry. By way of introduction, it is useful to first discuss the concept of collective memory and its importance.

The collective memory of a nation is that set of beliefs about the past which the nation's citizens hold in common and publicly recognize as legitimate representations of their history.[5] Collective memory is important because shared beliefs about the past provide citizens with common landmarks or examples which can be referred to when addressing the problems of the present. As in other nations, collective memory in America is structured through the political interaction of groups seeking to position themselves in relation to one another. Thus one way to demean another group is to deny the value of its history. Written out of the national past, the group is denied the collective landmarks which signify its importance. A public history which promotes negative views of a group, or simply excludes it from consideration, does real harm to the living members of that group.[6]

In our society the power of historical representation has largely been delegated to institutions such as museums, history sites, schools, and universities. These institutions exert enormous influence over the public perception of the past. A group's ability to control these institutions, then, will bring with it the power to determine both what history is publicly presented and how it is interpreted. At the time of Kennedy's inauguration, American minorities had little influence over the institutional representation of their past, but the transformation of American collective memory was soon to begin.

The black Civil Rights Movement achieved great successes with the Civil Rights Act of 1964 and the Voting Rights Act of 1965, but 1965 was also the year of the Watts riot in Los Angeles. And it was that riot, not the legislative achievements, which set the tone for the rest of the decade. Throughout the late 1960s, fires in American cities signaled that the nation had not put its house in order simply by changing its laws. Those who study social movements often describe post–1965 America as the time of the collapse and fragmentation of the organizations which made the Civil Rights Movement possible.[7]

This view is accurate but limited in that it defines political success solely in terms of changing laws or the structures of the State. If one focuses on culture rather than on law, significant achievements can be seen in the ferment of the late 1960s. People who lived through the era often say of themselves and the nation, "We were trying to figure out who we were." And in this statement we find the suggestion of an important pattern in the events of the time. This pattern becomes particularly clear when we consider the limitations of the legal revolution which immediately preceded the rioting.

American society in 1965 offered little public recognition of the value of minority cultures and identities. Worse, negative group images continued to legitimate a racial caste order in this country. While the Civil Rights Act of 1964 and the Voting Rights Act of 1965 dramatically expanded legal representation in America, those laws could do nothing to redress the cultural exclusion which continued. Just as the laws of the land had to change to include the politically disenfranchised, so too the cultural identity of the nation would have to change to include the culturally disenfranchised.

Beginning in the mid-1960s, a generation of minority activists turned to the task of gaining cultural representation. Black Power, which emerged in 1966, was the first expression of this cultural activism. Its adherents fought to change American perceptions of black identity, in large part by changing national perceptions of black history. Black Power, manifested in groups such as SNCC (Student Non-Violent Coordinating Committee), also inspired other minority groups to try to affirm their heritages. By the end of the 1960s similar identity movements developed among Indians, Asian Americans, and Latinos. New visions of the past were powerfully articulated by small groups such as AIM (American Indian Movement), Manzanar Committee (Japanese Americans), and Crusade for Justice (Chicano).[8]

The various assertions of minority cultural identity since the mid 1960s are referred to here as the Race Pride Movement. Race Pride was a diffuse movement comprised of relatively autonomous groups working toward the common goal of achieving national cultural recognition. While the activists of each racial and ethnic group sought recognition for their own particular culture, the net result of their efforts was the cultural transformation of a nation that had already experienced a major legal revolution. Moved by the rhetoric of groups such as SNCC and AIM, minorities activists carried the struggle for cultural inclusion into museums, history sites, schools, and universities. All across America, collective memory (conceived as the publicly presented past) was changed by people engaged in a cultural revolution which had no single leader, but which nevertheless dramatically transformed American identity.

Race Pride activists addressed institutionalized exclusion just as the Civil Rights workers had done, yet Race Pride has never been recognized as a distinct social movement. There are two reasons for this. First, the number of minority groups involved in the Race Pride Movement has prevented recognition of their common goal and collective achievements. The Civil Rights Movement was a predominantly black social movement, but virtually all minority groups contributed to the success of Race Pride. Because so many groups asserted their distinct heritages in the Race Pride Movement, it is

easy to lose sight of Race Pride's collective impact on American institutions of cultural representation.

Second, Race Pride's decentralized structure has made it difficult
to recognize as a social movement. The Race Pride Movement never
developed the mass membership organizations, such as the NAACP
(National Association for the Advancement of Colored People) and
SCLC (Southern Christian Leadership Conference), which were so
important to the success of the Civil Rights Movement. Intense cen-
tralization of resources was not necessary for the Race Pride movement's success because its targets—numerous museums, history
sites, and schools across the country—were individually less formidable than the primary target of the Civil Rights movement—the
State.[9] Although physical segregation, like cultural exclusion, existed
in countless places, the black Civil Rights Movement dealt Jim Crow
a death blow by destroying its supporting, centralized, legal framework. In contrast, the Race Pride movement generally had to address
institutionalized cultural exclusion one place at a time.

Despite its organizational diffuseness and diverse membership, a
basic pattern in the Race Pride Movement emerges. First, as with the
Civil Rights Movement, there was a period of agenda-setting and cultural awakening. Before Race Pride activists could go on the offensive, they had to ask some hard questions about themselves. In order
to counter white-dominated interpretations of American history,
these activists first had to decide what visions of the past they wanted
represented in the national arena. This was no simple matter of asserting self-evident truths that had been suppressed by white hegemony. On the contrary, the assertion of identity in the late 1960s involved the rediscovery of heritage by minorities themselves, intense
debates about which history mattered, and then more debates about
how to interpret that history. Second, after arriving at a particular
understanding of their history, individual activists and small groups
influenced by Race Pride attempted to transmit that vision of the past
to other members of the minority group and then to the nation as a

whole. Achieving national recognition was a long and arduous political process which involved expanding the representation of minority history in existing institutions, as well as creating new institutions to represent their past.

In the following chapters we will look at each of the four major American minority groups involved in the Race Pride Movement: Indians, Asians, Latinos, and blacks. In order to make the changes they wrought in American collective memory as concrete as possible, the focus of this work will be on changes in the American landscape itself. Thus particular attention is given to the creation or transformation of the national historic site most closely associated with each of the four minority groups: the Little Bighorn (formerly Custer) Battlefield in Montana, the Manzanar Internment Camp in California, the Alamo in San Antonio, and the Martin Luther King, Jr. birth home in Atlanta. Since so many people visit these historic sites, they constitute some of the most publicly accessible manifestations of the Race Pride Movement. Two of these case studies, the Little Bighorn and the Alamo, describe how minorities altered entrenched national interpretations of the past. The other two case studies, of the Manzanar and King sites, describe how minorities expanded national memory by creating new institutions of historical representation.

Each chapter begins with a description of the efforts of a minority group to define a positive heritage for itself. These accounts provide insight into how minority identities are constructed in contemporary America. Each chapter concludes with a case study of a specific political effort to present an affirmative image of minority heritage at a public history site. These examples illustrate in detail how Race Pride-inspired minorities have changed public historical representation through political action.

The various expressions of Race Pride emerged within a short period of time and were relatively autonomous. The chapters are therefore ordered by theme rather than by chronology. Chapter 1, on Indians, describes the relationship between racial identity revivalism and political efforts to alter national collective memory. Chapter 2, on Asian Americans, demonstrates that not all racial groups are capable of asserting a shared vision of their history, and that their members may opt instead for particular ethnic, rather than racial, self-conceptions and remembered pasts. Chapter 3, on Latinos, illustrates that it is sometimes impossible for an ethnic group to reach consensus on the nature of its identity and the content of its historical experience, and that this will limit the group's ability to influence the publicly remembered past. Chapter 4, on blacks, shows that while intense group solidarity is a major asset in attempting to influence American collective memory, such solidarity may also result in a collective forgetfulness of history that cannot readily be interpreted from the perspective of Race Pride.

Collectively, these chapters demonstrate that recognition of the role of minorities in American history has increased not because of a general drift toward cultural pluralism, as is often believed, but because of concrete actions which can be documented. This work may thus be conceived as a study of the production of a new American collective consciousness. The poet and novelist Robert Penn Warren once said that "to be an American is not . . . a matter of blood; it is a matter of an idea—and history is the image of that idea."[10] What follows is an examination of how that idea has been transformed by direct political struggle.

CHAPTER ONE

American Indians

We turn, all of us, to history for a sense of identity. To answer "American" to the question "Who are you?" is to evoke a set of images from the nation's past and a sense of one's own moral order and purpose. But the historical content of the American identity is a very selective recollection and ordering of past events, selective both individually and collectively. One person's memory need not be another's, nor need one group's memory be shared by other groups. So it is with the story of the Western frontier in American history. Tales of pioneers pushing back the wilderness call up images of heroism for many Americans, while memories of the same events evoke a sense of tragedy and regret in others. In both the heroic and tragic versions of frontier history, the American Indian plays a central role. This chapter examines how contemporary Indians have worked to change the popular memory of the frontier and their place in its history.

The Robert Frost and Maya Angelou inaugural poems of 1961 and 1993 illustrate the way the national memory of American Indian history has changed. In "A Gift Outright," Frost wrote that, before Northern Europeans moved West, the land was "still unstoried, artless, unenchanted."[1] Angelou, speaking from the perspective of the earth itself, presented different memories of the Indians and a different evaluation of their successors.

> You, who gave me my first name, you,
> Pawnee, Apache, Seneca, you
> Cherokee Nation, who rested with me, then

Forced on bloody feet,
Left me to the employment of
Other seekers—desperate for gain,
Starving for gold.[2]

The old frontier vision of progress equated the annihilation of Indians with the march of civilization. In this vision Indians represented the natural world. White men battled against this world, which they believed would envelop them if progress halted even temporarily.[3] Historian Richard Slotkin writes that for generations of Americans "the meaning and direction of American history . . . [was] found in the metaphoric representation of history as an extended Indian War."[4] Long after the historian Frederick Jackson Turner announced the end of the actual frontier in 1893, Americans continued to believe that progress justified, or at least made inevitable, the destruction of the Indians.

Such an image of the American frontier and of the Indians' position in it obviously placed living Indians at a cultural disadvantage. Popularly viewed as vestiges of a primitive time before North America became civilized, Indians had difficulty convincing other Americans of the value of their distinctive cultures in the present. For non-Indians, the frontier vision encouraged condescension or hostility toward any contemporary expression of Indian culture. Not surprisingly, those Indians who held on to their culture fared poorly in the generations after the end of the Indian Wars.[5]

Their low status remained unchanged through the first phase of the Civil Rights Movement. While the Voting Rights Act of 1965 ensured Indians access to the franchise, they constituted a majority in only a very few counties in America. Thus legal representation did not yield the kind of immediate political gains it did for blacks in some areas of the deep South.[6] Since the voting majority of Americans in virtually every area of the country did not value Indian identity, the Voting Rights Act made little impact. For significant change to take place in the status of Indians, general cultural attitudes about Indians would have to change. Since the 1960s, they have fought, like other minorities, to change the national recollection of their history and thereby alter the national attitude toward living Indians. As it turns out, Indians have been particularly successful in their efforts to influence American popular memory. This chapter describes how a small minority was able to improve its national status by promoting a different vision of the past.

Pan-tribalism and Collective Memory

Organized Indian opposition to national collective memory first emerged with the Red Power movement in the late 1960s. While Indians were not very involved in the earlier Civil Rights Movement, they, like many other groups, watched television and learned.[7] In particular, young Indians were moved by the assertions of heritage by Black Power advocates in the late 1960s. And like Black Power (described in Chapter Four), Red Power was concerned primarily with the recovery and assertion of an affirmative racial identity.

Indian scholar and activist Vine Deloria, Jr., explains that Red Power got its start among "[u]rban Indian activists seeking an Indian identity and heritage."[8] As they struggled to construct and assert a positive sense of group identity in a nation which had long disparaged them, urban Indians turned to certain symbols of the Indian past. In particular, they embraced symbols of Indian resistance to white aggression. At this point, "[t]he definition of Indian power began to take on a historic dimension, with appeals to the past glories of warriors such as Crazy Horse and Geronimo."[9] Becoming reacquainted with the fighting spirit of Indians in the past was thus one step toward constructing a vigorous Indian identity in the present.[10]

For many urban Indians, the reservations themselves represented a locus of Indian identity that they had never experienced. Thus, during the late 1960s and early 1970s, urban Indian activists worked to strengthen their ties with reservation Indians. Vine Deloria describes the results: "This contact sparked a tremendous interest in the tribal language and traditions, and many of the urban Indians began to show up on the reservations, seeking the tribal heritage they had been denied. They became the most militant of the advocates of cultural renewal."[11] Urban Indians gained a new sense of culture through association with the tribes. Reservation Indians, in turn, were radicalized by that association. Throughout Indian lands, the accommodationist policies of older tribal chairmen began to lose favor, particularly among younger Indians. The idea that the national government could be successfully resisted reemerged for the first time in generations.

Deloria writes that "[b]y mid-1972 the middle ground of progressive ideology in Indian affairs was fast eroding, and desperate confrontation was in the air."[12] The Indian movement that emerged in the early 1970s successfully brought together reservation Indians and their long-standing material grievances with urban Indians and their radical, though often heavily symbolic, interests and tactics.[13] Although a few tribes which had successfully continued to assert their rights as separate nations in the preceding decades, particularly the Hopi and Six Nations ("Iroquois"), proved less receptive to the idea of a pan-tribal movement, most tribes welcomed the urban radicals.[14] The Indian movement which emerged fostered a symbiotic relationship between urban and reservation Indians that has proved to be the basis for the gains made for all Indians in the last quarter century.

The Indian activism of the late 1960s and early 1970s gradually became more of a joint effort by urban and reservation Indians. One of the first pan-Indian demonstrations was the takeover of Alcatraz in 1969. Although dominated by urban Indians acting with no formal connection to any tribe, the seizure dramatized many long-standing Indian grievances, particularly federal violations of land rights granted to tribes by treaty. As the radicalism of the urban Indians continued to work its way through the reservations, larger joint efforts became possible. It was the 1972 Trail of Broken Treaties march which first brought large numbers of urban and reservation Indians into a dynamic coalition working toward many of the goals that had been articulated at Alcatraz.[15]

In October 1972 a group of Indian protesters calling themselves the Caravan of Broken Treaties set out from California for Washington, D.C., planning to arrive in the capital the week before the presidential election. The Caravan went through many Indian reservations en route, and many reservation elders joined.[16] When the Caravan, by then several thousand strong, arrived in Washington, the protesters were coolly received by the Bureau of Indian Affairs (BIA).[17] President Nixon and Vice-President Agnew both refused to meet with representatives of the group. Tensions flared and, after the riot squad was called, five hundred Indians forcibly occupied the BIA offices in Washington. Thirty-two Indians were charged with grand larceny and arson, though none were indicted.[18]

The Nixon administration "rejected the whole idea of treaty reform, on the ground that individual Indians had been made citizens earlier in the century and no treaties could be made with individual citizens."[19] The denial of sovereignty struck at the heart of both urban and reservation attempts to reassert meaningful Indian identity in the present. The government's refusal to consider the protesters' demands thus spurred the growing Indian movement. The most important expression of Indian activism in this century occurred soon after, with the takeover at Wounded Knee in 1973.

Wounded Knee

The central figure in the Wounded Knee takeover was Russell Means, an energetic urban Indian and leader of the American Indian Movement (AIM), an organization which had been founded in Minneapolis in 1968.[20] Means became involved with AIM at the time of the Alcatraz takeover, and he was later identified by the FBI as a main "radical element" in the Trail of Broken Treaties march.[21] His contribution to AIM's radicalism was considerable. In particular, Means understood how to dramatize Indian causes effectively for the general public.

In early February of 1973, Bureau of Indian Affairs officials became panicked in the face of growing unrest (and AIM influence) on the Oglala Pine Ridge Reservation in South Dakota. To shore up their position, BIA officials called federal marshals to Pine Ridge, the location of the Bureau's administrative headquarters on the reservation.[22] This was a terrible mistake, for Russell Means and the other activists instantly recognized the portentous historical parallel to the BIA's buildup of federal law enforcement, the Wounded Knee Massacre.

Wounded Knee, the most famous massacre of Indians in American history, was perpetrated on the Pine Ridge Reservation in the winter of 1890–91. Tragedy occurred when the troops of the Seventh Cavalry (George Armstrong Custer's old regiment) were called in after BIA officials became alarmed by unusual Indian activity on the reservation, what became known as the Ghost Dance movement. The ghost dances were a pan-tribal movement sparked by the Indian prophet Wovoka's vision that the world would soon end and then be reborn populated with buffalo and Indians, but no whites. Believing that the world would end when winter was over, ghost dancers performed a dance which Wovoka had seen in his vision. While unquestionably symbolizing a great threat to whites, the actual dancers themselves never organized to fight, for, after all, they believed that the world was about to end. When the Seventh Cavalry caught up with the Indians, the soldiers fired into a group which included many women and children, killing approximately half of the crowd of four hundred.[23]

Recognizing that a radical presence on the Oglala Reservation was once again causing federal officials to arm, Means, acting with the cooperation of most of the reservation's residents, decided that it was time to refight Wounded Knee.[24] Eighty years after that historic massacre, hundreds of AIM-inspired Indians, both locals and visitors, seized the little village, "announced the creation of the Oglala Sioux Nation, declared independence from the United States, and defined their national boundaries according to the Fort Laramie Treaty of 1868."[25] The time was right for Indians to make a point about the present and its relation to the past. Russell Means appeared on national television promising to shoot anyone who violated Indian territorial boundaries.[26] Galvanized by Nixon's snubbing of the Trail of Broken Treaties march, the Indians at Wounded Knee were heavily armed and emotionally ready for a fight.

The Federal Bureau of Investigation (FBI) was called in and the village quickly became a war zone.[27] The standoff was perfect for the media: Indians barricaded in the village where one of the worst massacres of their people had occurred; the federal government ready to attack them again. Gunfire was exchanged regularly for more than two months. Two Indians were killed, and an FBI agent was partially paralyzed.[28] Miraculously, the takeover ended with a peaceful mass arrest on May 9.[29] Although the Indians won no concessions from the government, their act of defiance was an important step in the reformation of Indian identity in America.

The importance of Wounded Knee for Indians cannot be overstated. Vine Deloria observed that because of the takeover, "Indians had developed a new pride in themselves which transcended tribal loyalties and instilled in Indian children everywhere the image of the brave Indian warrior, which had been missing in Indian society for two generations."[30] Both reservation and urban Indians were involved in the action and the experience gave both a new sense of direction.

The fact that the shoot-out occurred at the Wounded Knee site was especially significant for Indian identity. By successfully holding off federal agents for two months, modern Indians spiritually reclaimed Wounded Knee as a source of fighting pride rather than submissive shame. Deloria even claims that "Wounded Knee marked the first sustained modern protest by aboriginal peoples against the Western European interpretation of history."[31] Indians had challenged America culturally for generations by refusing to disappear, but the takeover of this historic site was their first direct assault on collective memory.

Ironically, Wounded Knee is now on its way to becoming a major federal historic site. The development of the site by the National Park Service has been slowed only by the Oglala's understandable reluctance to turn land over to any federal agency. (The site will be leased to the United States.) A separate effort has also continued for a formal apology from the U.S. government and monetary compensation for the descendants of the victims.[32] Claudia Iron Hawk Sully of the Wounded Knee Survivors Association expressed these demands in testimony before a Senate committee: "History has to be rewritten to show the Indian side. Apologies and memorials have to be made to the victims' descendants of [sic] the 1890 massacre at Wounded Knee."[33]

To summarize, Red Power originated in the identity needs of a generation of urban Indians who felt alienated from American culture and who turned to their Indian heritage for a better alternative. Reaching for a new sense of the past, they developed an active antagonism toward the mainstream representation of their history. Acutely aware of the connection between identity, history, and political power, urban Indians became increasingly active in the reshaping of American collective memory, often energizing reservation Indians in the process. The Wounded Knee takeover in 1973 was thus both a protest over treaty rights and a reclamation of the collective memory of the historic Indian struggle for justice. While it yielded no immediate material benefits for Indians, Wounded Knee was a turning point for modern American Indian identity, marking the maturation of both pan-tribalism and Indian political radicalism.

Since Wounded Knee, Indians have worked to replace the negative national memory of their various heritages with a more positive memory of Indian cultures and of their resistance to America's westward expansion. As Indians became more confident and aggressive, they took on bigger targets of traditional American nationalism. This soon brought them to an extended struggle to change the popular image of a man who had himself fallen to Indians a century earlier.

George Armstrong Custer

In 1876, at the Battle of the Little Bighorn, Indians killed George Armstrong Custer and all of his men. One hundred years later, the historian Brian Dippie observed that "[f]or Indians everywhere, Custer is the core of a complex of white racist beliefs."[34] Given that he was not a major Indian fighter and is best remembered for having had his entire command annihilated, why did Custer become so vilified by Indians?[35] The answer has to do with the popular (non-Indian) interpretation of Custer that developed after his death. For generations after the Last Stand, the annihilation of Custer's command was understood as a kind of blood sacrifice for American progress. Perhaps because his death came very near the end of the actual frontier period in American history, it seemed to cap an era. Custer was a martyr for the new industrial world, and his demise offered Americans a powerful warning about the dangers of falling back into a state of nature. Probably the best explanation for Custer's elevation to popular icon status is that his death reflected America's worst fears— the Indians got him, the chaotic world of nature enveloped him.[36] In any event, generations of Indians came to hate Custer less for what he did than for what he represented for non-Indians. And, in the late 1960s, they began to forcefully assert their own interpretation of Custer's life and the America of his day.

After Custer's death, his martyrdom was incorporated into the popular march-of-progress interpretation of the Indian Wars. In subsequent generations there were endless scholarly debates about his character and his military performance in the West before the Little Bighorn. These debates were bounded, though, by a general agreement that the Indian Wars were just or, at the very least, an inevitable cost of progress. Popular images of Custer, particularly as expressed in film, were very positive.[37] As long as general consensus about the justice of the Indian Wars remained, Custer's reputation was not seriously threatened.

It was not until the 1960s that this moral consensus finally collapsed. Then, for the first time, the goals for which Custer fought were generally questioned. In particular, Indian activists created a new and highly visible reinterpretation of Custer. Although more a political manifesto than a historical work, Vine Deloria's book, *Custer Died for Your Sins* (1969), signaled the real beginning of Indian efforts to change the popular memory of Custer. Instead of a sacrifice to progress, Deloria wrote, Custer "represented the Ugly American of the last century and he got what was coming to him."[38]

The year after Deloria's book appeared, Dee Brown came out with a work which would influence popular western historiography for the next twenty-five years, *Bury My Heart At Wounded Knee: An Indian History of the American West*. Brown's history includes an account of Custer's military actions in the West. Unlike previous authors, though, Brown offers no evaluation of the quality of Custer's military leadership. His critique starts and ends with a reassessment of the goals for which Custer fought. The defeat at the Little Bighorn is thus presented as partial recompense for the nation's mistreatment of Indians. Here at last was a new way of looking at Custer, one with the potential to end forever his traditional heroic image in popular culture.[39] Soon many Americans began to view Custer as an emblem of genocide and the rape of the West.

As Custer's goals were reexamined and found unjust, so too the man. In fact, his reputation has moved from one extreme to the other. One historian puts it bluntly, "Instead of demythologizing Custer, the Red Power activists have . . . [made] him the center of their own mythology."[40] Custer is thus a central figure in two radically different conceptions of American history, both ultimately structured to conform to prevailing racial attitudes.[41] Since the 1960s

changing perceptions of race in past and present society have reduced
Custer's image to an all-time low. As America's racial sensibilities
and values have changed, so too has our history.

A general value shift is not, however, a sufficient explanation for
the change in historiography that has occurred. Representation is
guided by power. Thus changes in representation must be described
as changes in the relative power of groups with competing visions of
the past and present. While Indians in the late 1960s and early 1970s
articulated very negative views about Custer, they did not have the
power to make the rest of America acknowledge the legitimacy of
their interpretation. This power could only be gained through political action. The cultural background which led them to this struggle
has already been described. What follows is an account of how Indians gained the power to present their interpretation of Custer to a
national audience. The focus will be on their struggle to control the
place most closely associated with him: Custer Battlefield National
Monument in Montana.

Custer Battlefield

Entering the Custer battlefield one is struck by the inherent drama of
the site. The road suddenly curves to offer a direct view of Last Stand
Hill. On the Hill, over a mass grave, stands a single white funerary
obelisk, distinctly out of place in the undisturbed gray-green chapar-
ral that surrounds it. The interpretation of this sacred American space
has changed over time, and these changes speak volumes about the
evolving racial conscience of the nation. In order to understand why
Indians struggled so long for control of the site, it is important to recall how the space was interpreted in the decades before the Race
Pride Movement came to Montana.

Even before the first flourishing of Red Power activism in the late
1960s, Indians made it clear that the very name "Custer Battlefield"
was offensive to them. Indians protested that they, after all, had won

the battle and should be allowed to choose the name.[42] In reality, of course, Indians had won the battle but lost the war and thus the power to interpret the battle. The fight with Custer was actually only one of several confrontations in the same area during two days in June of 1876. Participants in those other engagements, as well as Custer's widow, Elizabeth, remembered the whole series of conflicts as the Battle of the Little Bighorn, after the river which runs through the area. The historic park that the National Park Service operates there encompasses the site of the Custer battle and the sites of some of those other struggles (which the Indians also won). That the whole area was then named Custer Battlefield clearly signified to visitors that the meaning of the area revolved around Custer and what he symbolized. This was particularly upsetting to Indians, who preferred the morally neutral and historically more accurate nomenclature of the Little Bighorn.

Other features of the historic site made it clear that Indians were not welcome. Literally all of the stone markers in the area memorialized the army soldiers. No commemorative marker was ever constructed for the Indians.[43] In the most basic physical sense, they were nowhere to be seen. Moreover, the heroic version of the Custer story was related in great detail in a museum the Park Service constructed on the battle site.[44]

The National Park Service acquired the site from the War Department in 1940. The first and longest-tenured Superintendent of the site (1941–1956) was Edward S. Luce, a former Seventh Cavalryman and ardent Custerphile.[45] During his three years with the Seventh Cavalry (1907–1910), Luce had served with some of the same men who had fired on women and children at the Wounded Knee Massacre in 1890. His interpretation of Custer and the Seventh Cavalry was nothing short of worshipful. Luce supervised the construction of the battlefield museum and set the tone for the next several decades of interpretation. Under his administration the site developed into a Custer and Seventh Cavalry shrine.[46]

Even while the museum was still under construction, thousands of visitors poured into the site. Each received the official National Park Service brochure which explained the significance of the area. The first brochure from the mid-1940s set the tone for decades to come: "Although Custer Battlefield National Cemetery is a reminder of the struggle for possession of a continent, more specifically it commemorates the part the United States Army, ever obedient to the dictates of a democratic government, played in conquering the last frontier."[47]

As the visitor walked into Luce's Custer Museum, which opened in 1952, a "facsimile front page of the *Bismarck Tribune* was the focus."[48] The headline of the paper read simply, "MASSACRE." The next display was a diorama of the heroic Last Stand. While dramatic, the museum displays portrayed Custer and his men as pure victims. There was no suggestion that the army should not have been there in the first place. The Indian side of the story was poorly represented in a few displays such as "Indian Weapons" and "Hostile Indians." The only comment on Indian civilization came in a case labeled "Indian Medicine," which was intended to show "the importance of magic in the life of the Indian."[49] Suffice it to say, the museum was neither for nor about Indians. It portrayed the traditional vision of Custer as a martyr.

The remarkable thing about Luce's interpretation of the battle was that it lasted for so long. Even in the tumult of the late 1960s, it remained unshaken. Again a Park Service brochure presents the essential thesis: "The [Custer] National Monument memorializes the sacrifices and heroism of the United States Army in the conquest and pacification of the western frontier."[50] It was not until the early 1970s that this patriotic orthodoxy finally began to break apart.[51]

The Caravan of Broken Treaties, which wound its way toward the nation's capital in 1972, stopped at the Custer Battlefield in October. The visit was the beginning of organized opposition to the federal government's interpretation of the westward expansion. Russell Means, whose involvement in the subsequent Wounded Knee takeover was discussed earlier, came with members of the American Indian Movement. Means and his followers requested permission to place a memorial to the Indians who fought at the Little Bighorn, the first memorial of its kind. In particular, they proposed digging a hole into the mass grave of Custer's men and placing there a large metal plaque, which read: "In memory of our heroic warriors who defended our homes and lands against the hostile aggression of the US government."[52] The superintendent at the time, Eldon Reyer, refused permission to place the plaque but was supportive of the proposal to expand interpretation to include Indians. He also agreed with Means that the site's name should be changed. Reyer explained to a local reporter: "I think he'll be coming back through to help us more. His ideas were good ones."[53] Reyer sounded enthusiastic about revising the site's interpretation, but little changed during the rest of his administration.

AIM's demonstration did, though, inspire some of the site's staff to generate proposals for a new interpretation. While hardly as radical as what Means wanted, the proposals were a first step. They suggested "that interpretation at the battlefield begin with a program on the Custer myth; and that the focus of *all* programs be the 'clash of cultures.'" New programs would be designed to address three questions: "What became of the Plains Indian? What did the nation gain in the Plains Indian wars? Can violence in cultural conflicts be avoided?"[54]

These proposals, which seem moderate enough today, were greeted with violent internal opposition. One staff historian described the plan as an "interpretive jihad," arguing that the Park Service "must not take sides in historical events" and that "Custer Battlefield is not the proper place to attempt to discuss . . . white-Indian conflict in North America." He believed that including the proposed themes would be a misguided attempt to "right social wrongs" by revising the past. Robert Utley, the assistant director of interpretation for the National Park Service, agreed. Utley wrote that the Park Service was not "capable of properly addressing the subject of Indian-white relationships."[55]

Utley had been a staff historian at Custer Battlefield and his reaction to the reform proposals could have been predicted from his earlier writings. In 1968 his interpretive handbook for the battlefield was published. The book contained virtually no information on the Indians and began: "On a hot June Sunday in 1876, hordes of painted Indian warriors—perhaps as many as 4,000 [sic]—swarmed over a treeless Montana ridge."[56] Whatever interest in interpretive change Russell Means's followers generated in 1972, the Park Service administration was not prompted to action. Such reform would not begin for several years.

Park Service memos from that time give the impression that most of the people who resisted interpretive change at Custer Battlefield during the 1960s and 1970s believed that Russell Means and other Indian activists were part of a broad antinational campaign, that they were there to criticize America. While this was undoubtedly true, the deeper meaning of Means and the AIM movement was the struggle for a positive Indian identity. What Indians wanted at Custer Battlefield was not merely recognition that cultures had clashed there. Rather, Indians wanted a frank admission by the federal government that, in that historic struggle, *the Indians were right*. Such a change would entail more than the rejection of American nationalism, it would require a complete revaluation of Indian identity in America.

In the wake of the Wounded Knee takeover a year later, interpretive change finally began at Custer Battlefield, though not for the best of reasons. Fear of violence at Indian history sites grew. In particular, potential problems with the upcoming centennial of the Last Stand loomed large. Recognizing the possibility of conflict, a Nixon staff member wrote the Park Service warning that the "consequences of an unsophisticated treatment of that occasion could be portentous."[57] Raymond Freeman, acting associate director of the Park Service, agreed that the centennial services "must not emphasize the Indian-white man conflict that existed in 1876 *and still exists today.*"[58] From then on, the Park Service began to back away from strong expressions of nationalism at Custer Battlefield.

Freeman suggested that conflict at the upcoming centennial might be avoided if the Park Service dropped its nationalist rhetoric at the site and interpreted the battle as a "historic event, rather than a racial conflict."[59] Race had figured prominently in the march-of-progress interpretation, and racial conflict also dominated the Indian view of American history. But Freeman suggested that the Little Bighorn should be presented as a military encounter that had no wider meaning beyond the battlefield itself, especially in regard to race. As such, the conflict would be interpreted as something that "just happened."

The focus in the new interpretive approach to the Indian Wars would be on the details of the fighting.[60] For the Park Service, an emphasis on pure military history had the twin virtues of being unassailably objective and utterly value-neutral. This shift to military history reflected a moral crisis in the Park Service. Increasingly aware of popular dissatisfaction with patriotic orthodoxy, and unwilling to pursue any alternative, the agency fell back on rhetoric about objective history.

"Objective history" has long been a catch phrase in the Park Service, and it has had different meanings in different contexts. First, and most simply, when the unwritten assumptions of a historical interpretation have gone unchallenged for long periods, then that interpretation has been deemed objective. The "winning of the West" interpretation was thus considered objective during the period when there seemed to be national consensus on the meaning of that period in American history. But, in times of crisis, objective history has had another meaning. When faced with criticism of the values it was attempting to assert, the Park Service retreated into a kind of empiricism that is drained of significance.[61] Thus, during the years after Wounded Knee, the Park Service limited its interpretation to what could be known with near certainty, the details of the fighting.

The Park Service's decision to interpret the battle strictly as a military encounter had a direct effect on the plans for the proposed centennial celebration at the battle site in June of 1976. Thousands of people were expected to show up for the occasion. Fearing ideologues of any stripe, the Park Service worked hard to spoil its own party. With the takeover at Wounded Knee in mind, an FBI Regional Special Events Team was called in. They began patrolling the area in May and continued through the anniversary. Racial tensions in the area increased and poisoned any hope for a positive Indian-white dialogue at the centennial. The Park Service also worked to deflate the centennial by shifting the official memorial services from the actual date of Custer's defeat, Saturday, June 25, to Friday, June 24. The plan worked. Instead of a crowd of many thousands, only eight hundred attended. While the date switch effectively avoided a large crowd, those who cared most still showed up: white Custerphiles and Indian revisionists.

The official memorial services drew an audience of about five hundred. During these services AIM activists arrived. "Some in the mainly white audience uttered a low sound of apprehension as more than 100 Indians walked . . . toward them."[62] Russell Means calmed Superintendent Hart, explaining: "We've done our fighting. We're here to celebrate."[63] While the whites made their speeches, the Indians continued up the hill to the Custer Monument. They danced around the mass grave singing in Dakota, "Custer Died for Your Sins." Later they reminded the site manager of their continuing desire to see the name of the site changed. Means told Superintendent Hart, "I couldn't imagine a Lt. Calley National Monument in Vietnam." Hart, wanting to get the Indians to go away, accepted the Vietnam analogy and responded, "Neither could I."[64] The demonstration was the first time in a hundred years that Indians had held a celebration at the site of one of the greatest Indian victories.[65]

Back down the hill, official observances were calculated to be uninspiring and succeeded. The tone of the official observances was set by the battlefield's site manager, Richard T. Hart: "The Custer Battlefield is today a national monument, administered by the National Park Service as part of the nation's historic heritage. It exists not to take sides on the Battle long past, but to preserve and present the story."[66]

Robert Utley, representing the national offices of the Park Service, offered a stronger statement on behalf of objective history: "The stereotype of the Indian prevalent in my youth encouraged a false and one-dimensional view of the marvelously rich and diverse culture of the American Indian. Today's stereotypes of pioneer and soldier are equally false and simplistic."[67] Utley also challenged the audience to embrace historicism: "They [the soldiers] belonged to different cultures. They had different attitudes and beliefs. They were of another time . . . We do not have the obligation, we do not even have the right, to indict these people—or to forgive them for that matter—for actions that may be offenses according to the standards and perceptions of today but were not according to those of yesterday."[68]

Utley eloquently expressed the Park Service's desire to avoid imputing meaning to the American past. His plea for neutrality was politically naive, though. Indians wanted a frank admission that they had been treated unjustly. They sought to indict the people who had taken so much from them. Without a national admission that they had been wronged, Indians inevitably felt that their identities in the present were disparaged. They understood that without recognition of the value of their history and culture, general advancement in American society would remain difficult for them. By convincing Americans that they had been treated unjustly, Indians hoped to improve their status in contemporary society. Utley's historicist orientation denied Indians the moral high ground of the past and a major resource in their struggle for justice, and thus generated nothing but resentment.

This resentment showed up in other events. In 1976, Congressional hearings prompted by the Wounded Knee takeover in 1973 sought to reevaluate the meaning of the 1890 massacre. The hearings also attempted to determine whether or not there were grounds for providing reparations and an apology to the descendants of the massacre victims. Robert Utley testified for the Park Service in opposition to both. As he explained to a reporter, the attack on women and children was "just something that happened."[69] There was, of course, no way to convince the children and grandchildren of people killed at Wounded Knee that the deaths of their family members "just happened." Though Utley suggested that the soldiers had panicked and thus were not to blame for the killing, Indians could not have cared less for his reasoning. Hearing this explanation from a prominent white Custer historian only aggravated the sense of wrong they already felt. Utley believed that, by backing away from the nationalist verities and patriotic orthodoxy that once surrounded Custer, the Park Service interpretation would be both more objective and more palatable to Indians. Indians did not see it that way. From their perspective both the old patriotic orthodoxy and the new Park Service historicism fundamentally denied that Indians were a people who had been wronged.

While American society tore itself apart in the early 1970s, the Park Service kept its head down. At Custer Battlefield, Utley's historicist vision continued to inform the official interpretation. Responding to Indian activism, the Service pulled back from assertions of traditional patriotic orthodoxy and burrowed into military history. Many of the historians who worked there convinced themselves that the detailed focus on military history represented the cutting edge of objective history. In this view they were encouraged by their contact with another group devoted to Custer's memory, the Custer Battlefield Historical & Museum Association (CBHMA).

The Park Service had always been attuned to the attitudes of Custerphiles and nationalists because of a unique cooperating agreement which existed with the CBHMA for decades. The group was founded in 1953, under the Luce administration, as a private club for

Custer buffs, with the administrative function of operating the bookstore at the battlefield museum and thereby generating revenue for specific park projects.[70] For decades the relationship was cozy enough, but, as America began to change in the late 1960s and early 1970s, the Park Service became aware that it was institutionally attached to a fiercely nationalistic historical association. When the Service tried to back away from both patriotic orthodoxy and the hero-worship of Custer, the Custer Association criticized it publicly.[71]

Regarding CBHMA criticisms as a threat to its institutional autonomy, the Park Service in 1976 tried to "dilute the influence of the association by the infusion of large numbers of members, widely scattered around the country. This they believed would make the group much easier to control."[72] Opened to national membership, the ranks of the CBHMA swelled from fewer than 50 to almost 3,000. Not surprisingly, almost all of those who joined were Custer fans and violently opposed to any changes at the battlefield. Thus, instead of weakening the organization, the Park Service turned it into a national lobbying group committed to maintaining Custer's image at the site. However, the Park Service soon discovered that the CBHMA could be largely placated by an exclusive focus on military history, a hobby of most Association members.

The history of the CBHMA reveals much about why change occurred so slowly at Custer Battlefield. Originally created to serve the Park Service, the volunteer organization became a state-supported lobby for a particular vision of the past. The CBHMA national office was located near the park and its employees worked in the bookstore at the battlefield. In contrast, many of the Indians who were active in the earlier protests had to drive hundreds of miles to get to the site. While some interest had always existed in the Park Service for changing the interpretation of Custer, it became harder than ever for its proponents to develop concrete plans for change. Without major local support it was unlikely that the Park Service would become pro-Indian.[73]

The CBHMA powerfully influenced Park Service interpretation for the next decade. Had the Association not had so much local influence, Park Service personnel might have independently moved to meet the demands of Indians. In his classic study of organizational co-optation, *TVA and the Grass Roots,* Philip Selznick observed that "[c]ommitment to existing agencies may shape and inhibit policy in unanticipated ways."[74] So it was at Custer Battlefield. Captain Luce's old organization continued to exert a strong influence long after the passing of its founder and his world view. It would take more than another decade of Indian activism to break its hold on the site.

In the 1980s, local opportunities for Indian reinterpretation appeared dim. The superintendent of Custer Battlefield for most of that decade, Jim Court, maintained the site's close relationship with the CBHMA. One Indian observer, reflecting back on that period, claimed that Court ran the site as "a playground for Custer buffs."[75] Court alienated local Indians by helping to found the private Custer Battlefield Preservation Committee (CBPC). The Committee was created for the purpose of raising money to buy nearby property for the National Park Service. Local Crow Indians interpreted the move as a land grab and protested at the 1987 anniversary. During that small protest, the Indians went so far as to denounce Court on the park's public address system. One protester also used the opportunity to express hostility toward the Park Service's interpretation of the battle: "There should be a monument there, you know, Cheyennes, Arapahos, Siouxs [sic], there should be a monument there for the people . . . [E]verything is Custer, everything."[76]

Court left the site in 1988. The brief tenure of his replacement, Dennis Ditmanson, was punctuated by a very important Indian protest: the return of Russell Means and the American Indian Movement. Previous AIM demonstrations in 1972 and 1976 had been peaceful. Their relative moderation compared to the 1973 Wounded Knee takeover no doubt encouraged the Park Service's inertia. In 1988 AIM returned with the intention of redirecting the interpretation of the site and making their vision stick. Means came to the 112th anniversary of the battle with a group of about forty AIM activists. He told Ditmanson that earlier park managers had promised the placement of an Indian monument at the site and supported changing the site's name.[77] Nothing had been done. Now, Means said, Indians realized that they had been betrayed by the Park Service.

Means gave a speech to the crowd in which he attacked white civilization for the horrors it had wrought. Referring to Custer's men, he said that "eighty percent of the soldiers shot themselves because they were drunk," and that the soldiers actually outnumbered the Indians.[78] Means pointed at the National Park Service museum and exclaimed, "The whole thing is a lie! My heart bleeds when I think of people in that place."[79] Turning to the Custer Memorial, he said, "Can you imagine a monument listing the names of . . . Nazi officers erected in Jerusalem? A Hitler national monument?"[80]

At the end of Means's harangue, a group of his followers came forward and dug a hole in the mass grave of Custer's men.[81] Into this they poured pre-mixed cement, in which they set a plaque which read: "In honor of our Indian Patriots who fought and defeated the U.S. Calvary [sic]. In order to save our women and children from mass murder. In doing so, preserving rights to our Homelands, Treaties and Sovereignty."[82] One commentator on the incident writes that Indians "had escalated symbolic guerrilla warfare beyond protest to physical intrusion at a patriotic gravesite."[83] The historic site was once again at the forefront of the debate over the content and meaning of American collective memory. The way in which Means reopened debate is significant. By laying the plaque on the grave of Custer's men, Means and his followers were not just protesting the absence of Indian representation at the site, they were appropriating the site for their own purposes. Heretofore Park Service officials had thought that by focusing solely on the military conflict they could avoid the larger cultural issues. The Indians' violation of the mass grave dramatized their profound dissatisfaction with "objective" military history.

By 1988, popular support for the re-interpretation of the West was clearly greater than it had been in the mid-1970s. In an opinion poll conducted by the Park Service after the Indian plaque was installed, the vast majority of respondents favored either leaving the plaque where it was or creating a freestanding monument to the Indian warriors. The self-administered form naturally over-represented those who felt strongly (pro or con) about the plaque. Still, the responses were surprisingly positive. A couple from Kentucky wrote: "We were deeply moved by the plaque. [The] words are extremely eloquent, relevant and essential. The warriors who died there were Americans, too, real Americans. The plaque should remain—Please bolt it down."[84]

In the 1970s, in the face of Indian protest, the Park Service had hidden behind military history. This time they took the Indians' side. In retrospect, it might seem obvious that the Indians were going to win their fight to change the meaning (and name) of Custer Battlefield. For years, though, the Custer Battlefield Association's lobbying efforts had prevented the Park Service from making changes. The CBHMA's vocal presence at the site caused the Park Service to grossly overestimate the public's support for the military history approach. By the late 1980s, Americans were little inclined to champion the cause for which Custer fought, and few people shared the Park Service's fascination with military history. Thus, following the initial placement of the plaque in 1988, Indians won a series of victories that resulted in a complete interpretive transformation of Custer Battlefield. Considering the inertia of the previous decade, these changes occurred with impressive speed.

Shortly after 1988, institutional changes occurred at Custer Battlefield which prefigured future developments in interpretation. Most important was the appointment of Barbara Booher as superintendent of the site. Booher was not only the first woman appointed, but also the first Indian. She enthusiastically supported changing the name of the site to Little Bighorn and erecting an Indian monument. During her four-year tenure Custer Battlefield was remade.

With real local and institutional support for their ideas, Indians were now able to move ahead with great speed. In 1990 a bill to establish an Indian memorial would have passed both houses of Congress but for the last minute addition of a provision which would have changed the name of the battlefield. Because Montana's two representatives split on renaming the site, the bill died. The next year, in 1991, there was a new bill (H.R. 848) supporting the name change and the memorial, this time with better organization and agreement among Montana's representatives. The governor even sent a letter of support. Ben Nighthorse Campbell (D-Colorado, now R-Colorado), who claims to be a descendant of a warrior who fought at the Little Bighorn, vigorously championed the bill.[85] Hearings that year revealed massive support for the bill. Public meetings in Billings, Montana, in June brought out over two hundred people. Eighty-five percent of those attending supported both the Indian memorial and the name change. Most of those opposed were from the area around the battlefield and were afraid that the change to the less familiar Little Bighorn would affect tourism.[86]

Some opposition to the bill came from traditionalists over the next few months, but they were largely a dispirited group. The Custer Battlefield Association polled its membership and dutifully reported that they supported an Indian monument but not the name change. George Armstrong Custer IV, a direct descendant of General Custer, worked tirelessly to prevent the change, but was able to influence only one vote. A selection from one of his editorials gives real insight into the wider meaning of the name change.

He has indeed become the nation's scapegoat for the guilt we feel about our country's failed Indian policies of the past and present . . . Have we come to putting the blame on one man? Can we so easily shift the guilt of society to one individual? Proponents of H.R. 848 say yes. But wouldn't the nation's anger be more appropriately vented towards the politicians of the day? Discredit the Indian policy of the nineteenth century, but do not dishonor an American soldier who gave his life executing that policy.[87]

As Custer IV rightly noted, the public demonization of Custer had by the late 1980s become an easy way for Americans to demonstrate their racial enlightenment, in the process completely exaggerating Custer's historical significance and, perhaps, culpability.

Custer IV's lobbying had little influence. Only one dissenting vote was cast in the House, by John Dingell (D-New Jersey). Dingell agreed that the bulk of the testimony "demeaned" the soldiers.[88] In the Senate only Malcolm Wallop (R-Wyoming) voted nay. The thrust of his testimony was summarized in one line: "We could avoid the whole problem and confusion by simply living with history as it was originally written."[89] More caustic was the testimony of Lowell Smith of the Little Big Horn Association, a group devoted to the worshipful memory of Custer: "Totalitarian states practice historical revisionism. They simply tear down monuments and rewrite their history. But democratic societies do not change their history."[90] However, the vast majority of testimony was in support of the name change and highlighted its importance for American Indian identity. Ben Nighthorse Campbell described what Indians felt before they reasserted pride in their past.

> For generations now the accolades paid to General Custer and the valor attributed to him, let alone that a national monument bears his name, has [sic] been like a slap in the face to many Indian people in the United States who survived or descendants of people who survived those harsh times. Many of them feel like they have been treated like second-rate citizens and often as pawns or bait to attract tourists to western historic locations.[91]

The Morningstar Foundation, an Indian lobbying group, submitted testimony about how Indians interpreted the battle: "It is because of the valor and sacrifice of the past generations of all Indian nations in defense of treaty, sovereign, and human rights that there are any Indian people alive today. The heroism of our relatives at the Battle of Little Bighorn has become the symbol for Indian people generally of the just and provident actions of all our ancestors to protect family and home."[92]

The National Park Service was also unequivocal in its support of the changes. Robert Utley, who had previously described the massacre at Wounded Knee as something that "just happened," spoke eloquently on behalf of the bill. His testimony is that of a man who had seen the American mind change and had made peace with it: "The national values and attitudes expressed by the existing monument have changed radically in the past century—indeed in the past quarter century. The military focus of the monumentation at Custer Battlefield is offensive not only to Indian people but to all citizens who believe in the cultural pluralism that has embedded itself so firmly in the present generation of Americans."[93]

In the end, nationalist platitudes and value-neutral military history were both rejected in favor of a frank recognition that the Indians had been right to resist the invading Americans. H.R. 848 sailed through both houses virtually unopposed and delivered a clear mandate to the Park Service to change the interpretation of the battlefield.[94] The interpretive fight which ended in 1991 was as complete a victory for the Indians as that on the Montana battlefield more than a century before. The victors of the Battle of the Little Bighorn had at last won the power to write its history.

At the site itself, the name change had an immediate impact on park attendance: Indians started coming. As the staff archivist, Kitty Deernose, explained, "Back in the old days an Indian or two would come into the visitor's center, and kind of look around with this 'Can I come in here?' look. Now many are coming."[95] Barbara Booher said, "I can see it out my window, and it never used to be that way."[96] Indian visitation has at least tripled in the last five years, accounting for as many as 40,000 of the site's 400,000 total.[97] Encouraged by the name change and visitor reactions, Booher hired more Indian interpreters and thereby changed, in a basic physiognomic sense, the appearance of the whole site. The front desk in the visitor center is now often staffed exclusively by Indians. Where ten years ago there were only white faces, the new Indian staff proclaims, by their physical presence, "Welcome to an Indian history site."

The Future of the Past

The congressional vote on H.R. 848 was a formal expression of a shift in the balance of power of historical representation. That the final vote was nearly unanimous suggests that by 1990 Indians had gained substantial power over the representation of their past. While the power shift is clear, it did not produce a clear blueprint for action. Indians gained control of the Little Bighorn, but not a plan for what to do with the site. It was not clear, for example, what connection, if any, would be made between the interpretation and the racial identity of the people doing the interpreting.

In the past, interpretation at Custer Battlefield was overwhelmingly dominated by whites. Booher, in turn, aggressively hired more Indians. The possibility of a new segregation—that is, an all-Indian staff—quickly appeared. Booher's replacement as superintendent was Gerard Baker, a reservation-born Indian with personal commitment to Indian issues. In conversation, Baker reflected on the forces that had propelled the name change and were now encouraging site segregation. Referring specifically to urban Indian intellectuals, he said: "Their way of identifying and helping the cause, if you will, is to bring up the Little Bighorn and say 'You need all Indian staff here. You need all Indian language here. You need all Indian interpretation here.' OK, but that hurts everybody else."[98] Because the political struggle to change Custer Battlefield was driven by the strong identity needs of American Indians, the new officials may repeat some of

the mistakes of the 1950s by moving to the opposite interpretive extreme, in this case typecasting white people as evil or all Indians as
living in paradise before whites arrived. Already the site shows a film,
Last Stand at the Little Bighorn, which portrays Custer as merely a symbol of racism. Further, in 1996 Gerard Baker invited Indians to celebrate the 120th anniversary of Custer's defeat by riding horses to the
federal soldiers' mass grave and counting coup, that is, hitting the
century-old obelisk with sticks.[99] Some observers questioned
whether this action was indicative of a new double-standard for historical representation. One asked, "What would people say if cavalry
re-enactors went to Wounded Knee and touched the monument [to
the Indian dead] with sabers?"[100]

These issues are not unique to the Little Bighorn site. As Indians
have gained greater control over the representation of their past, the
concomitant responsibilities have posed serious problems that never
arose when they were shut out of power. More than ever, Indians
have to face tough decisions about how to define their history. The
problems and possibilities of a 1990 law, the Native American Graves
Protection and Repatriation Act (NAGPRA), illustrate this challenge.
NAGPRA gives Indian tribes the power to take back from American
museums any article which an Indian tribe regards as sacred or a central piece of its cultural patrimony.[101] Barbara Isaac, associate director of Harvard's Peabody Museum, explains what this legislation
means both for her museum and for living Indians. "There are challenges both for the museums and the Indians in this act. For the museums there will be the extensive labor of inventory building, and the
verification of shelf items against lists. But for the Indians the verification will be on what is central to their culture, and what is sacred.
This is a spiritual verification, and much more demanding of integrity
and clarity of vision."[102] Under NAGPRA, museums will have to take
contemporary tribal self-definitions seriously, precisely because those
tribes are now empowered to seize objects from their collections.
And as Isaac explained, this new law also carries with it the expecta-

tion that Indians will define their heritage. That is, for museum professionals to respond to the new power of Indians, Indians must decide what in their culture is really sacred. For those Indian tribes which have lost nearly all of their traditional identities, such self-definition may prove difficult. Having achieved considerable power over the representation of their past, they must now ask some very hard questions about its meaning. The potential gain is great but, as the excesses of earlier white historiography illustrate, nostalgia and ethnocentrism are temptations for all empowered peoples.

Conclusion

Through political action Indians have achieved considerable influence over the historical representation of their cultures. The struggle at the Little Bighorn suggests that the change in memory Indians so desired occurred only because they kept fighting for it. Even after the general American interpretation of the West had shifted in their direction, it took active and even violent protest at the Little Bighorn to alter the meaning of the past presented there. Thus, what might appear to be just a manifestation of general cultural evolution must also be understood as the result of specific political actions.

Local politics can have a great influence on the interpretation of national sites. It was the massive support of Indians on the Pine Ridge Reservation which made possible the sudden and violent disruption of meanings traditionally associated with Wounded Knee. And, at the former Custer Battlefield, the ability of the National Park Service to reflect changing national attitudes was severely compromised when they were effectively co-opted by an organization (the CBHMA) which they had created in a different era. Without strong local support for the interpretive change they desired, Indians had to work long and hard to achieve their goals.

The goals of these struggles over collective memory were informed, however, by the interaction of local activists with the wider national culture. Urban Indians were profoundly attuned to the identity crisis of America in the late 1960s, and they were the first Indians to develop the identity implications of the Race Pride Movement. These urban Indians understood that the new, post-1965 frontier for minority advancement would be the struggle for cultural self-definition. In their efforts to reclaim their racial identity, urban Indians like Russell Means reinvigorated their sense of connectedness with the centers of traditional Indian identity—the reservations—where they rekindled a sense of fighting pride that had been missing in Indian life for more than a generation. Ironically, it was those Indians who were most assimilated who sparked the revival of militant Indian ethnicity.

One of the main goals of Red Power was to revise the popular memory of the Indian in American history. Generations of Americans had been taught that the destruction of Indians was an inevitable part of the manifest destiny of the nation. With a deep sense of the injustice inherent in this vision of the past, Indians fought to replace patriotic orthodoxy with their own version of history. A strategic part of that fight was for control of specific historic sites like Wounded Knee and the Little Bighorn Battlefield. The details of those conflicts illustrate that concerns of group identity and group power often converge on physical space itself. They show that changes at those historic sites are produced by, and constitutive of, shifting group power relations in American society.

Institutional changes at the Little Bighorn Battlefield and NAGPRA legislation have given Indians considerable power over the interpretation of their history in the institutions of American collective memory. In fact, they have gained such control over their past that they have effected a virtually complete reversal of American attitudes toward Indians. Where Indian identity was once disparaged, it is now actively sought. This is demonstrated by the U.S. Census, which indicates that, since the 1960s, hundreds of thousands of Americans who had previously identified themselves as white have reidentified themselves as Indians.[103]

CHAPTER TWO

Asian Americans

Collective memory reflects the interests of the present. In fact, a direct relationship can often be found between a contemporary group's needs and how the group remembers the past. One of the central concerns of this work is to demonstrate that since the mid-1960 minority groups inspired by Race Pride have asserted histories which affirm their identities. Another concern is to show that the concrete sociological differences between these groups are reflected in the sorts of histories they have produced. In the case of Asian Americans, patterns of recent immigration have set strong limits on efforts to affirm a shared sense of racial identity and heritage, so that the greatest successes have come from constituent ethnic groups.

To explain the ways in which Asian Americans have been involved in the Race Pride Movement, it is necessary to review some basic demographic information. Between 1970 and 1980 the number of people of Asian ancestry in America more than doubled, growing from 1.5 to 3.5 million. By 1990 the population had again more than doubled, reaching 7.3 million, the majority of whom were immigrants.[1] These immigrants have come to a country in which the meaning of race has changed dramatically in the last generation. The 1965 Immigration and Nationality Act ended much of the discrimination in immigration policy and made possible the influx of Asian immigrants in the past two decades. And in 1975 the legal protections of the Voting Rights Act were extended to Asian Americans.[2] Thus the millions of Asian immigrants who have arrived in the last two decades have found a much more tolerant society.

This change of racial climate has naturally influenced the way Asians conceptualize their identity in America. In particular, the amelioration of racial oppression in this country has created a situation in which the lived experience of many people is not so powerfully shaped by race. Without constant racist coercion, most members of the various groups which constitute Asian America now tend to think of themselves in specifically ethnic terms, as Chinese Americans, Korean Americans, Japanese Americans, and so on. Awareness of a shared Asian racial identity is episodic; it informs Asian Americans' self-understandings at specific times but has not become a stable way of seeing the world. In times of crisis, though, race does become a meaningful category.

For example, the murder of Vincent Chin caused a variety of ethnic groups to band together politically as Asian Americans because of shared concern about anti-Asian racism. At the time of his death, Vincent Chin was a twenty-seven-year-old Chinese American draftsman. One night in June of 1982, Chin stopped at a Detroit bar with a few friends. Things turned ugly in the bar and a patron yelled out, "Because of you . . . we're out of work."[3] Apparently mistaking Chin for Japanese, some men in the bar started a fight. Chin and his friends ran out of the bar and became separated. Two of the men from the bar caught Chin in the street and beat him to death with a baseball bat—one man holding him while the other man swung. Arrested at the scene, both men were convicted of homicide without premeditation and manslaughter. Each was fined $3,000 and put on three years' probation. Outrage at the light sentence led to the creation of the American Citizens for Justice (ACJ), a pan-Asian group organized for the purpose of having Chin's assailants tried in a federal court for civil rights violations.[4]

From her study of the ACJ and other organizations that developed after Chin's death, Yen Le Espiritu concludes that "it is anti-Asian violence that has drawn the largest pan-Asian support."[5] Predictably, nothing creates a coalition among the various ethnic groups of Asian

America faster than racial violence.[6] When specific racial problems arise, the term Asian American takes on meaning it does not have in ordinary life. Irene Hirano, Director of the Japanese American National Museum, explains that Asian American is "a political term, not something that is [individually] internalized."[7] Thus Asian American does not refer to a constant experience of shared culture and values, but rather to a political alliance which forms at specific moments. For individuals, the term Asian American also comes to life on government forms and college applications which ask about racial identity. America's fascination with race (and enduring racism) occasionally force individuals of Asian ancestry to emphasize their physiognomy.[8] But the forces of racialization have thus far proved weak: Asian Americans continue to regard themselves primarily as ethnics.

These basic realities of Asian Americans—being predominantly an immigrant population in a nation where racial oppression has diminished—constitute the limits within which efforts to promote a pan-Asian American consciousness must operate. If the needs of the living influence the remembrance of the past, then the absence of a shared contemporary culture among Asian Americans is certainly a serious obstacle to the development of a pan-Asian consciousness. However, we must be aware that there are individuals and institutions which are specifically devoted to creating this racial consciousness. In particular, we need to examine the efforts of activists to use the American past to promote a sense of group identity among all peoples of Asian ancestry.

As in the case of Vincent Chin, the racism of the American past could logically serve to promote a sense of racial consciousness among Americans of Asian ancestry. After all, for a good part of their 150-year history in this country Asian Americans have been targets of racial aggression.[9] The Chinese Exclusion Act of 1882 set a precedent for the National Origins Act of 1924, which prohibited Japanese immigration. Both, in turn, were informed by the same racial attitudes which culminated in the mass imprisonment of Japanese Americans during World War II. Because America's treatment of Asian Americans (almost all of whom were of Chinese, Filipino, or Japanese ancestry) through the 1960s was terrible, the past itself is a resource which some activists and intellectuals have tried to use to promote a sense of group identity among contemporary Asian Americans. Yen Le Espiritu, a professor of ethnic studies, explains the work of individuals like herself: "The construction of pan-Asian ethnicity involves the creation of a common Asian-American heritage out of diverse histories. Part of the heritage being created hinges on what Asian Americans share: a history of exploitation, oppression and discrimination."[10]

The obvious problem with this reasoning is that most Asian Americans have immigrated to this country since the mid-1960s and thus do not share a common history of exploitation in America. Further, almost half of the new arrivals are from countries previously unrepresented in America, and for them America's past mistreatment of people of Chinese, Filipino, or Japanese ancestry has little resonance.[11] Toward the end of her work on pan-Asian identity, Espiritu meditates on this problem and appears to contradict her earlier assertions about a shared past:

> Since the pan-Asian concept was forged in the late 1960s, the Asian-American population has become much more variegated. The removal of racial barriers in the economic sector and the preference for highly educated labor in immigration legislation have increased the ranks of educated professionals, thus fragmenting Asian Americans more clearly than in the past along class lines. The post-1965 immigration has also brought new ethnic constituencies into the pan-Asian fold, many of which are unfamiliar with or indifferent to the pan-Asian concept. Coming from different worlds, the post-1965 Asian immigrants and the American-born (or American-raised) Asians do not share a common history, sensibility, or political outlook. With-

out shared world views, collective modes of interpretation, and common class interests, the prospects of a viable pan-Asian ethnicity appear bleak.[12]

As Espiritu explains, the pan-Asian concept first flourished during a time when Japanese and Chinese Americans still constituted the majority of the Asian American population. (Filipino Americans were not so active in the pan-Asian movement.)[13] It was Japanese and Chinese Americans, with relatively small immigrant populations in their midst, who were inspired by the rhetoric of Race Pride. Because this work seeks throughout to demonstrate the impact that Race Pride had on collective memory, it is worth reviewing the period during which pan-Asian thought actually flourished outside the confines of university Ethnic Studies departments.

Asian Race Pride

Pan-Asian identity activism (sometimes described as Yellow Power) developed in the 1960s, a little later than Red Power and Black Power, but it was especially vigorous because of the way it was linked to the Vietnam War protests. The perception that Vietnam was a racist war provoked questioning of previous engagements in the Pacific. Activists quickly recognized that America's actions in the Pacific have always had racist overtones. The army slang expression "gook," for example, had been heard many times before Vietnam. First used in reference to Filipinos during the Philippine-American War (1899–1902), the term survived into the Korean and Vietnam wars. Similar racial denigration of the enemy was common during World War II. Observing America's historical tendency to conceptualize overseas Asian enemies in racial terms, it was a logical next step for activists to look back at how America had treated its citizens of Asian ancestry in the past. Opposition to the Vietnam War thus instigated a search for the historical content of the Asian American experience.

According to William Wei, resistance to the Vietnam War touched off a search for "a common Asian American identity rooted in a past history of oppression and a present struggle for liberation."[14]

It was during the Vietnam War that students began their push for the establishment of Asian American studies programs in universities, mostly in California.[15] Wei explains that these programs, while representing a net expansion of knowledge within the universities, were created to address "the identity crisis of Asian American students."[16] The programs that were established met this crisis by "reviewing their [Asian Americans'] historical roots . . . especially their oppression by European American society and their resistance to it."[17] By looking back to their past experiences in America, rather than to their nations of ancestral origin, Asian Americans "acknowledged a distinct Asian American identity that had evolved over the years."[18]

During the late 1960s it was easier to organize these pan-Asian efforts because the great wave of Asian immigration of the 1970s and 1980s had not yet occurred. In 1970, Asian American still meant mostly Japanese and Chinese American.[19] Both groups had long histories in this country and could find a common ground. They were able to form, in Ronald Takaki's expression, "a community of memory."[20]

The mass immigration of the 1970s and 1980s has, as Espiritu reluctantly concludes, derailed for now the development of any pan-Asian consciousness. Still, the efforts to develop a race-based cultural identity in the America of the late 1960s and early 1970s are of interest for two reasons. First, Asian American identity activism initially followed the Indian pattern, where different tribal identities came together in a pan-tribal movement to assert a shared vision of racial identity and heritage. If not for mass Asian immigration, the term "Asian American" might today signify a coherent group identity based largely on shared memories of oppression in America. Second, although the efforts of Asian Americans (mostly of Chinese and Japanese ancestry) during the 1960s and 1970s have not resulted in the creation of a coherent racial identity, Asian ethnics inspired by Race Pride have had a significant influence on national collective memory.[21] This is illustrated by the case of Japanese Americans, who will be the focus of the remainder of this chapter.

Japanese Americans and World War II

Beginning in tandem with the early Vietnam War protests, Asian Americans sought to reassert memories of their mistreatment in the American past. In doing so they inevitably came to question the received popular wisdom about the meaning of certain eras in American history, most notably the dominant national memory of World War II. Because World War II holds such a prominent place in American collective memory, it is useful to see in detail how Japanese Americans, originally inspired by Race Pride and pan-Asian consciousness, have worked to transform America's memory of that period.

Given that World War II is perhaps the event of this century in which Americans have taken the greatest pride, the issue of memory may not seem problematic. Its designation as "the Good War" implies that it was unambiguously moral. The actions of the Germans and the Japanese clearly justified our fighting in Europe and the Pacific. In contrast to America's frontier history, the heroes and villains of World War II remain obvious.

That this image would be passed down to future generations was the fervent wish and expectation of many Americans who lived through that period. Since the late 1960s, however, Japanese Americans have worked to memorialize their experience of World War II, an experience which casts some shadow on that otherwise illustrious time. In particular, Japanese Americans have worked to preserve the memory of the U.S. government's mass internment of Japanese-American citizens during the war. Because the camp experience is still not common knowledge, we need first to review a basic outline of the internment.

The Internment

In 1981 Dillon Myer, then ninety years old, made a last wish: "I do not want to go down in history as a director of concentration camps."[22] To the end the Ohio-born bureaucrat maintained his belief that the agency he headed during World War II, the War Relocation Authority (WRA), had been an "exciting adventure in the democratic method."[23] Although it is easy to lose sight of the WRA in that seemingly infinite number of Roosevelt-era acronyms, few who know its history would give the same rosy description: the WRA was the agency which managed the imprisonment of virtually everyone of Japanese ancestry living on the West Coast at the outset of World War II, incarcerating some 120,000 Japanese citizens and American citizens of Japanese ancestry.[24]

The idea of imprisoning the entire Japanese American population living on the West Coast developed in the aftermath of Pearl Harbor. Two weeks after the attack, Lt. General John L. DeWitt, leader of the Western Defense Command in America, proposed the roundup of all Japanese, German, and Italian citizens residing in the United States. The latter two groups included many people who had come to this country to escape the Nazis and Fascists. As time progressed, DeWitt's plan became limited to just the Japanese, but expanded to include not only Japanese citizens (40,000 people) but also American citizens of Japanese ancestry (an additional 80,000).[25] The roundup of citizens was authorized by Franklin Roosevelt's Executive Order 9066 of February 19, 1942. Asked about the legality of detaining citizens, DeWitt explained: "A Jap's a Jap. They are a dangerous element, whether loyal or not. There is no way to determine their loyalty . . . it makes no difference whether he is an American;

theoretically he is still a Japanese and you can't change him . . . by giving him a piece of paper."[26] President Roosevelt may have agreed to the roundup because he believed it was a military necessity or acted in a panicked response to the attack at Pearl Harbor. Although the military necessity never existed, the panic that gripped the nation was real enough and certainly contributed to his support for the plan.[27] The evidence also suggests an uglier reason for FDR's Order: Roosevelt and his Secretary of War, Henry L. Stimson, held certain racist beliefs about Asians in general and Japanese in particular.[28] In his diary, Stimson recorded the following observation on Japanese Americans and Executive Order 9066: "Their racial characteristics are such that we cannot understand or trust even the citizen Japanese . . . [This] is the fact but I am afraid it will make a tremendous hole in our constitutional system to apply it [9066]."[29] And Executive Order 9066 did indeed make a tremendous hole in the Constitution. The heart of the Order read:

> [B]y virtue of the authority vested in me as President of the United States, and Commander in Chief of the Army and Navy, I hereby authorize and direct the Secretary of War . . . to pre-scribe military areas in such places and of such extent as he or the appropriate Military Commander may determine, from which any or all persons may be excluded, and with respect to which, the right of any person to enter, remain in, or leave shall be subject to whatever restrictions the Secretary of War or the appropriate Military Commander may impose in his dis-cretion.[30]

Before the Order was released the press was informed that, despite the vague wording, 9066 would only be applied to people of Japanese ancestry.[31] One of the supreme ironies of Roosevelt's administration is that Executive Order 9066 was issued shortly after Executive Order 8802, which was one of the most racially progressive actions of the first half of this century—8802 barred discrimination in defense industries for any reason of "race, creed, color, or national origin."[32]

In March of 1942 Roosevelt created the War Relocation Authority to enforce 9066.[33] The President then picked the WRA's first director, Milton S. Eisenhower, younger brother of Dwight D. Eisenhower. Although Eisenhower was not excited about his role in the war effort, he accepted the assignment and went to work immediately. Imprisoning 120,000 people was an enormous undertaking.[34] Eisenhower and the WRA were charged with constructing the prison camps while the military rounded up the people. Over the next month General DeWitt issued a series of Civil Exclusion Orders designating the Japanese for internment. In order to make sure that West Coast Japanese Americans did not leave the area, DeWitt issued Public Proclamation No. 4, which prohibited voluntary evacuation from Military Area No. 1 (the West Coast). The roundup went very smoothly. First DeWitt would issue an Exclusion Order for a given area, for instance, a section of Los Angeles. The Order would then be posted in public places and people of Japanese ancestry would typically have between two to seven days to report. During this time they had to sell all of their household items, including vehicles. Many had to abandon their homes, others had to sell them at a great loss.[35] Family fortunes were lost in the rush.

Residents of a given target area were told to report to a particular location, often a fairground or racetrack, for relocation. These transitional locations were frequently not so transitional. Many citizens of Los Angeles, for example, spent months sleeping in the stables of the Santa Anita racetrack before being sent to the camps. The camps themselves were placed in remote locations in order to keep the supposed enemies away from sensitive military installations. By early June of 1942, General DeWitt announced that the military had removed over 100,000 people of Japanese ancestry, most of them U.S. citizens, to WRA centers. By August an additional 10,000 were taken.[36] The story of one family typifies this dehumanizing experience: "Henry went to the Control Station to register the family. He came home with twenty tags, all numbered 10710, tags to be attached to each piece of baggage, and one to hang from our coat lapels. From then on, we were known as Family #10710."[37] In mid-June of 1942, after the roundup was essentially complete, Milton Eisenhower resigned as director of the WRA. To his credit, Eisenhower had great misgivings about the whole affair from the beginning. In a letter to Secretary of Agriculture Claude Wickard he wrote, "when the war is over and we consider calmly this unprecedented migration of 120,000 people, we as Americans are going to regret the unavoidable injustices that may have been done."[38] Eisenhower left, but the WRA continued until 1946 under the direction of Dillon Myer, a former colleague of Eisenhower's from the Department of Agriculture.

Before he accepted the directorship of the WRA, Myer had a conversation with Eisenhower which throws considerable light on Myer's character and the meaning of the whole camp experience: "I asked Milton if he really thought I should take the job, he replied, 'Yes, if you can do the job and sleep at night.' He said that he had been unable to do so. I was sure that I could sleep, and so agreed to accept the position."[39] Though he did not want to "go down in history as a director of concentration camps," it is clear from his own account that Myer willingly participated in a massive violation of civil rights. Although the exact meaning of that violation is still debated, some sense of the internment can be effectively communicated with a few details.

It is the camp experience, not just the roundup, which forms the heart of modern Japanese American memory of World War II. The ten camps that Eisenhower established are today pilgrimage sites for Japanese Americans. They are scattered west of the Mississippi, in Rohwer and Jerome, Arkansas; Gila River and Poston, Arizona; Granada, Colorado; Heart Mountain, Wyoming; Minidoka, Idaho; and Topaz, Utah. The largest camp was at Tule Lake, California and the most famous, and first established, was at Manzanar, California.

The mass internment is perhaps most familiar today through the photographs Ansel Adams took at the Manzanar camp and published in the book *Born Free and Equal* (1944). The book's incendiary text (the epigraph is the Fourteenth Amendment) sounded the wrong note in war-excited America. Few copies were sold and many of those were publicly burned. The photographs, which have survived and been reissued, are a sad commentary on America during the Good War.[40] They show people living in sheet-metal barracks in an isolated corner of the Mojave Dessert. Altogether, tens of thousands of Americans sat out the war in places like Manzanar, living on an unfamiliar diet in locations chosen for their isolation. Surrounded by barbed wire, soldiers, and machine guns, children went to school and life went on, however dehumanized, for three years. Fifty years later, many people who were there still say, "I was in camp during the war."

Ironies proliferated during the camp experience. In early February 1943 the U.S. Army activated the 442nd Regimental Combat Team. The unit was composed of Hawaiian Japanese Americans (formerly the 100th Battalion) and Japanese Americans from the mainland who had volunteered.[41] Most of the mainland volunteers were men who had been placed in the camps, many of them after volunteering to fight in World War II or having already served in the military. By enlisting, many young men were able to escape the camps, but they had to leave their relatives behind. One of those volunteer soldiers later had to return to Manzanar to bury his younger brother—one of the two men killed in a food riot at the camp. It is a point of Japanese-American pride that the 442nd became one of the most decorated combat units in American history. One member, Sadao S. Munemori, won the Congressional Medal of Honor for saving his fellow soldiers by jumping on a hand grenade. His mother waited out the war at Manzanar. In a WRA publication applauding the regiment's persistent heroism, President Roosevelt was quoted as saying, "Americanism is not, and never was, a matter of race or ancestry."[42]

The Japanese surrendered in August 1945, and the last internment camp was closed in March 1946. President Harry Truman subsequently presented Dillon Myer the nation's Medal for Merit for his fine performance as director of the War Relocation Authority. The recommendation for the Medal, written by the Secretary of the Interior, Harold Ickes, is significant because it expresses the official interpretation of Myer and the camp experience. "By his scrupulous adherence to democratic concepts in his administration of the War Relocation Authority, Dillon Myer has established a precedent for equitable treatment of dislocated minorities. In doing so, he salvaged for American democracy a minority group that has proved itself well worth saving, and at the same time he saved the United States from jeopardizing its standing as a democracy in the eyes of other nations."[43]

Interestingly, a number of government officials, including Ickes, did not support the official interpretation. After the WRA camp program was transferred to his Department of the Interior, Ickes "peppered the President with letters asking that the internment and exclusion programs be ended, to which Roosevelt responded with vague assurances that he would keep Ickes's view in mind."[44] Ickes wrote the President on one occasion that "the continued retention of these innocent people in the relocation centers would be a blot upon the history of this country."[45] He also made a contribution to Adams's *Born Free and Equal,* copies of which he personally sent to Roosevelt.[46]

The same year that Ickes wrote Dillon Myer's letter of recommendation, he elaborated on a sentiment repeatedly expressed to Roosevelt.

Crowded into cars like cattle, these hapless people were hurried away to hastily constructed and thoroughly inadequate concentration camps, with soldiers with nervous muskets on guard, in the great American desert. We gave the fancy name of "relocation centers" to these dust bowls, but they were concentration camps nonetheless, although not as bad as Dachau or Buchenwald. War-excited imaginations, raw race-prejudice and crass greed kept hateful public opinion along the Pacific Coast at fever heat.[47]

The official interpretation of the internment was, then, hardly maintained by all the key participants. More than anything else, though, most Americans wanted to get this ugly incident behind them, to forget it. It would be the Japanese Americans who would have to keep the camp experience alive in national memory. And it is to their efforts to maintain public memory of that injustice that we now turn.

Memory and Manzanar

Although it was a defining life experience for a generation of Japanese Americans, the internment camps were not talked about much after the war. In fact, many children of camp internees never learned about their parents' ordeal until the 1960s, when the camps became an important subject in the developing study of Asian American history. One internee explained the generational dynamic of the war memory in this way: "There's a curious anomaly in our subculture which goes something like this: those of us who lived through the camp tend not to talk about it, about any sense of outrage. Within our community the parents never talked about what happened here with their children."[48]

It was not until long after the war that the camp experience began to receive attention, principally from younger Japanese Americans. In the late 1960s, Sansei (third-generation Japanese American) students began the long process of recovering the memory of the internment. Their efforts to have internees bear witness about the past were slowed by these individuals' natural unwillingness to talk about an experience that had been personally humiliating. The Asian American movement of the late 1960s and early 1970s facilitated the expression of those memories by encouraging internees to view the public statement of painful memories as a political act, one which promoted group empowerment. Each act of remembrance contributed to the larger group's efforts to make the rest of America see that the so-called "model minority" had suffered terribly in America.[49] Although the Asian American movement later collapsed under the weight of immigration, the historical consciousness of Japanese Americans was profoundly influenced by the brief flourishing of Asian Race Pride activism. This can be demonstrated by examining the early organized efforts to assert memories of the camp experience.

An important foundation for the movement to recover memory was the internee reunions, which began in the late 1960s. The first of these occurred in 1969, when a group of Asian Americans from California made the first modern pilgrimage to Manzanar, the most famous of the internment camps.[50] The pilgrimage was intended to dramatize support for the repeal of the Emergency Detention Act of 1950, a McCarthy-era law which "permitted the attorney general to apprehend and place in detention camps any persons or persons he suspected of . . . engaging in acts of espionage or sabotage."[51] The law included "provisions for the establishment of detention camps at locations such as Tule Lake, which was used during the Internment."[52]

In the furor of the late 1960s black activists and civil libertarians were the first to call attention to the lingering threat of the Emergency Detention Act.[53] Asian American radicals soon joined these other groups in organizing for repeal. This movement naturally took on a special significance for Japanese Americans. At Manzanar and other camps, Sansei students dramatized the dangers of the Detention Act by recalling the Japanese American camp experience. By memorializing that history the activists began to make Manzanar into an active site of historical memory for all Japanese Americans.

The first pilgrimage to Manzanar was a traumatic experience for many of the activists. The pilgrimage occurred on a bitter December day in 1969. Many students coming from Los Angles and San Diego had no idea of winter conditions in the higher elevations of the Mojave Desert. Standing in sub-freezing weather and looking out at a landscape of complete desolation, the students, many of them children of internees, experienced a profound communion with the past. The activists realized the magnitude of what had happened there and how little they had ever known about their parents' experiences. One speaker, Jim Matsuoka, reflected on the denial of the past that the internees had experienced for the last twenty years: "When people ask me, 'How many people are buried in this cemetery?' I say a whole generation is buried here. The Nisei Americans [second-generation Japanese Americans] lie buried in the sands of Manzanar."[54] The Nisei who went with the Sansei (third generation) students to Manzanar became symbols of the effort to assert Japanese American identity by reclaiming the past. Together, they fostered the hope that personal and group memories might enter the national consciousness by means of mass politicization.

A group of Japanese Americans quickly established the Manzanar Committee. The Committee's initial aims were to educate people about the camp experience and to organize support for making Manzanar a California state landmark. Problems with the landmark idea brought Japanese Americans to their first conflict with the government over the interpretation of the past.

California's Historic Landmark Advisory Committee granted Manzanar historic landmark status in January 1972, but difficulties emerged when it came time to decide what the plaque to be placed there would actually say. Here divergent interpretations of the camp experience clashed. The Japanese Americans proposed a plaque text that was unacceptable to the director of the California state parks system, William Penn Mott. The proposed text of the plaque read:

In the early days of World War II, 110,000 of Japanese ancestry were interned in relocation centers by Executive Order No. 9066, issued on February 19, 1942.

Manzanar, bounded by barbed wire and guard towers, was the first camp confining 10,000 persons, the majority being American citizens.

May the injustices and humiliation suffered in these concentration camps as a result of racism, hysteria, and greed never emerge again.[55]

Mott objected to the plaque on a number of counts. He wanted to delete the words "racism" and "greed" from the last sentence and substitute "relocation center" for "concentration camp."[56] In short, he preferred a more euphemistic interpretation of the internment experience. Mott agreed that there was in fact a regrettable wartime "evacuation," but felt that it was simply the result of wartime hysteria, nothing deeper.[57]

About this time, many of those who had implemented the internment order spoke in favor of the euphemistic interpretation of the past which Mott advocated. Dillon Myer, former director of the camp system, published his own account of the camp experience in 1971. For Myer, the camps were properly called relocation or evacuation centers.[58] He further argued that the camps were necessary to protect the Japanese Americans from likely assaults by white Americans.[59] Myer also claimed that the camps' work-release programs had facilitated Japanese assimilation by disrupting entrenched living patterns.[60]

A different sort of commentary on the camp experience came from the WRA's first director, Milton Eisenhower. In his 1974 autobiography, *The President Is Calling,* Eisenhower wrote of the internment, "I have brooded about this whole episode on and off for the past three decades, for it is illustrative of how an entire society can somehow plunge off course."[61] Eisenhower, though, also resisted the Japanese Americans' "concentration camp" nomenclature. He explained, "We called the relocation camps 'evacuation centers' . . . Never did we think of them as concentration camps."[62] California

Park Director Mott did not want to champion the WRA as Myer did, but he resisted the idea that American racism had run wild during the Good War. Thus, Mott continued to work to maintain a euphemistic interpretation of the past. Toward that end, he stalled the Manzanar memorial plaque for over a year.

At the Manzanar pilgrimage in 1972, Sue Embry, the chairwoman of the Manzanar Committee, spoke about the connection between Vietnam and the memorialization efforts at Manzanar: "With or without a landmark, Manzanar represents the ultimate negation of American democracy—that racism which today polarizes our country and its people and even as I speak, wings its message of destruction across the skies of Vietnam."[63] Emboldened and politicized by the anti-Vietnam War movement, Japanese Americans continued to push for their version of the past. Their efforts were also spurred on by Director Mott's callous request for "documentation to prove that racism and greed were involved in the evacuation."[64] Stonewalled, the Manzanar Committee and members of the Japanese American Citizen League (JACL) enlisted the aid of California Assemblyman Alex Garcia and Speaker Robert Moretti, as well as several other state senators. In a closed-door meeting with Mott and other involved parties, Garcia and his colleagues told the park director that there would be action in the state legislature if he continued to resist the plaque wording. Sue Embry explained, "[Mott] had no choice. The controversy would have gone to the state legislature and embarrassed [him]."[65] After well over a year of pushing, the Japanese Americans got the wording—and thus the interpretation—they preferred.

While yielding only a state landmark with a plaque, this first successful effort to assert their negative memory of the Good War affirmed contemporary Japanese American identity by winning official recognition of past injustices. Japanese Americans had proved that they could assert their collective memory of the past, and that opposition to their views would not be very spirited. After all, Mott had not fought the Japanese Americans' wording once the issue became public. Had he been truly committed to Myer's vision of the past, a real fight would have ensued. Mott, like Eisenhower, wanted to forget an embarrassing past. But, while this resistance to Japanese American memory was weaker than it would have been had state officials believed in the justice of the internment, the forces of forgetfulness could still exert much influence. The advocates for Japanese American memory learned this in their next major effort to represent their experience of World War II.

The next stage of memorialization was to have been the creation of a state park at the Manzanar site. At the time of the landmark designation, Speaker Moretti helped pass a resolution calling for a feasibility study for the state park. In September of 1974, the State of California Department of Parks and Recreation issued its report. It called for some reconstructions at the site, including a barbed-wire fence and guard tower to evoke the atmosphere of the time.[66]

Opposition to this proposal was well organized even before the plan went public. Worried that reconstructions at Manzanar might be presented in such a way that "would exaggerate the actual conditions that existed there," Parks Director Mott slowed the release of the study.[67] Opposition was strongest in Inyo County, where Manzanar is located. The locals objected vehemently to any reconstruction. Keith Bright, an Inyo County Supervisor, was one of many who opposed the planned reconstruction. As he explained it, "The plan was totally unreasonable, it would have made Manzanar look like Dachau."[68] With strong local opposition and a tight state budget, the park proposal died.

Despite this local setback, the national movement to remember the camp experience grew during the 1970s and early 1980s. In fact, it proved much easier to make progress in Washington, D.C., than at the local level in California. The main goal during that period was the Campaign for Redress, a movement to have the U.S. government issue an official apology for the internment and make a cash payment to each living internee.[69] The first step was the repeal of Executive

Order 9066, still technically valid after more than thirty years. Responding to the Asian American legislators in the House and Senate, President Ford issued his own Proclamation repealing FDR's order. In the Proclamation, Ford referred to the internment as a "setback to fundamental American principles."[70]

Although this apology was easily won from an establishment which had never taken any pride in the internment, Ford's proclamation provided national historical legitimacy to Japanese Americans' memory of the camp experience. Recognition of this new legitimacy came from the Senate in 1980, when it established the Commission on the Wartime Relocation and Internment of Civilians (CWRIC), charged with reconstructing the history of the camp experience and making recommendations for possible reparations.

Although there were already many scholarly works on the subject, the CWRIC held its own hearings and took testimony from camp internees. The Commission's efforts produced *Personal Justice Denied* (1983), a thick volume which now stands as the official government interpretation of the internment period. Significantly, the report addressed the reasons internment occurred, which Ford's apology had not done: "The promulgation of Executive Order 9066 was not justified by military necessity, and the decisions which followed from it . . . were not driven by any analysis of military conditions. The broad historical causes which shaped these decisions were race prejudice, war hysteria and a failure of political leadership."[71]

On the basis of its own documentation of injustice, the Commission recommended a formal apology and a payment of $20,000 for each survivor. Redress was supported by a strong majority in the Senate and the House, and the Reagan administration's opposition proved half-hearted. Assistant Attorney General Richard Willard publicly rejected the findings of the Commission, however. In hearings held in 1987 on whether or not to accept the Commission's recommendations, Willard sounded remarkably like Director Mott of California: "It may be that the [Commission] is correct in concluding that the assumptions on which the exclusion and detention programs were based were erroneous. It is a long unsubstantiated further step, however, to brand those actions as a product of racial prejudice, or hysteria and a failure of political leadership."[72]

Congress did not agree with Willard and accepted the Commission's recommendations in the Civil Liberties Act of 1988 (H.R. 442), which passed by a vote of 243–141 in the House and 69–27 in the Senate.[73] Many of the dissenting votes, cast by Republicans and Democrats alike, reflected concern about the price tag.[74] Sensing the ideological conviction that informed the majority vote, the Reagan administration reversed its opposition to Redress. President Reagan signed the Act, which promised a formal apology, and authorized payment of $20,000 for each survivor. President George Bush later signed appropriation bills which provided 1.65 billion dollars for those reparations.[75]

The Movement for Redress energized Japanese American activists throughout the late 1970s and 1980s. The government responded to their demands by rewriting the official history of the internment period and providing reparations to thousands of people. The enthusiasm generated by the Redress Movement's success also encouraged a redoubling of efforts to memorialize the physical sites associated with the camp experience.

During the 1970s and 1980s, the sites of the old camps continued to deteriorate. This posed an obvious danger to the memory of the camp experience. As geographer David Lowenthal has rightly commented, "A past lacking tangible relics seems too tenuous to be credible."[76] Soon the physical spaces associated with the internment might disappear and with them one of the strongest reminders of that history. As late as 1988, the year of the Civil Liberties Act, a scholar of public commemoration still found it necessary to write: "Perhaps the greatest shame is the federal government's absence of recognition for these places. The nation's misdeeds are not matched with dignified memorials which properly remember these camps. As war memori-

als, the camps have become increasingly invisible. The lack of attention to these sites has become a way to cover shame just as the dust or
overgrown vegetation has covered the reality of the camps."[77] While
the physical condition of the sites was poor in 1988, the federal government's acceptance of responsibility for the internment of Japanese
Americans provided the groundwork for a national effort to restore
the most famous of the internment camps, Manzanar.

To understand the wider significance of the preservation of Manzanar, one must have some general knowledge of the other efforts to
preserve World War II memories. The most obvious difficulty the
country faced in commemorating the war was that only one of the
battle sites, Pearl Harbor, was in the United States. That site was
memorialized by placing a large structure in the water above the
sunken USS *Arizona,* and in 1980 the memorial entered the National
Park Service's collection of historic sites. For the rest of the battles,
those concerned with preserving the memory of World War II understood that future generations of Americans were unlikely to travel
to obscure spots in the Pacific Ocean, or Europe for that matter.
Thus it was clear that wartime memories would have to be represented in civic memorials in America. For example, the enormous
Marine Corp War Memorial erected in Arlington, Virginia, in 1954
provided heroic representation of the valor of the soldiers in the
war.[78] Likewise, historic preservation of war-related structures was
to focus, of necessity, on domestic history sites. In 1984 the National
Park Service proposed that one of these, the Manzanar Internment
Camp, be included in its collection of national historic sites.[79]

Although the idea generated understandable enthusiasm among
Japanese Americans, the Park Service warned that it was not capable
of ensuring congressional approval of the plan by itself. Dan Olson,
author of the Park Service proposal for the Manzanar site, reflected
on the limits of the agency's legislative influence: "The future of the
proposal is in the laps of the general public and their elected representatives. If there is no concerted lobbying effort by the Inyo

[County] supervisors, local congressman, or the general public I can assure you nothing will happen."[80]

Establishing a national park, especially a historic site, customarily requires that the Congressional representatives from the state in question support the proposal. Because national parks bring federal money to states, it is rare that a historic site will generate state-level opposition. But as Olson understood, Manzanar might well prove an exception to the rule. The Japanese American internment was by any reckoning one of the worst violations of American civil rights in this century. National historic sites traditionally have been chosen because they reflect positively on the American experience. Whether it be Gettysburg or Kitty Hawk, a National Park Service site will generally celebrate the American character.[81] By contrast, Manzanar suggests that American history has not been a simple march of material and moral progress. Moreover, since the state historic park proposal had been stopped in the 1970s, it was reasonable to expect some sort of local opposition again.

From the first announcement of the Park Service proposal, Japanese Americans, energized by the Movement for Redress, pursued the proposal vigorously. While the Park Service spent the next few years generating the supporting documents for a formal site proposal to Congress, Japanese Americans associated with the Manzanar Committee worked to ensure that the local political climate in Inyo County would be favorable to the final legislation. Particularly instrumental in this regard was Rose Ochi, the pro bono legal counsel for the Manzanar Committee.

Ochi spent World War II in an internment camp in Arkansas and by the 1980s had become an established political figure in Los Angeles.[82] She helped ensure the passage of a bill (H.R. 543) authorizing the Park Service to acquire and develop the site by working out the local politics. Among other things, she met with local politicians to persuade them of the desirability of the park, especially as a tourist attraction.[83] Ochi's efforts were facilitated by the weakened opposition of aging World War II veterans. Moreover, local opposition largely dissipated during a public hearing on the proposal held in Inyo County in June of 1987, when Ochi brought two members of the 442nd Regimental Combat Team, Stephen and Noel Kabayashi, to the meeting. Veterans opposed to the national park turned out as predicted but were surprised by the presence of the two uniformed and decorated Japanese American veterans. Rather than the racial confrontation many had expected, the public meeting developed into an exchange of reminiscences.[84]

Ochi also befriended longtime Manzanar opponent Keith Bright. She persuaded Bright to support the park, but he remained convinced that the new memorial should not involve any site reconstruction, something he had always opposed. Bright, in turn, helped secure the support of California Senator John Seymour.[85] While there was legally nothing to prevent the Park Service from restoring the site to its original appearance, the process of making the site a national park was facilitated by assurances that no such restoration would occur. The National Park Service also encouraged local cooperation by deciding to interpret the entire history of the Manzanar area, including its Indian heritage (which pleased local Paiute Indians) and its pioneer heritage (which pleased some older white families).[86]

Using the legitimating rhetoric of the "stream approach" to historic site interpretation, the Park Service offered to talk about the multiple tragedies that occurred in the Manzanar area before the Japanese prison camp: most of the Indians were kicked off their land by the pioneers, and then the pioneers were kicked off the land by the Los Angeles Division of Water and Power during its enormous land acquisitions in the Owens Valley in the 1910s.[87] In fact, because of Los Angeles's water-rights maneuvering, the town of Manzanar had ceased to exist more than a decade before the internment camp was constructed. A few families from old Manzanar continued to live in areas close to the town's former site. Not surprisingly, they were delighted by the Park Service's suggestion that the history of the de-

struction of their town be told. Thus the Park Service's efforts to gar-
ner local support for the site produced a proposal to tell the story of
the mass victimization of Indians, Japanese Americans, and whites.
Every group's claim to victim status dutifully honored, local opposition largely ceased.

By the time the proposed Manzanar memorial finally came to a
vote in Congress, Redress had already passed and the site proposal
went through with ease. President Bush signed H.R. 543 into law on
March 3, 1992. He had previously signaled his support for the bill,
stating that the "wartime internment was a tragic mistake."[88] The
President put money into that vision of history when he signed the
appropriation bill for the camp internees' compensation.

Making Sense of the Past

Now that Manzanar is a national historic site new questions about
how to interpret the camp experience arise. That is, the Japanese
Americans' fights to preserve Manzanar and achieve Redress were
predicated on simply winning national recognition for past wrongs.
Having achieved this, Japanese Americans are now faced with the
complex issue of interpreting their own actions during the camp experience. Divisions within the Japanese American community's reaction to the internment pose particular problems of memory. For example, the interpretation of the Japanese American role in the
American military is a subject of contention. During the war, the
American government offered to release fighting-age men who volunteered for combat duty. It is difficult to know how to interpret the
differences between those who chose to fight and those who did not
(often called "No-No Boys," after a loyalty oath the government administered). This difficulty is especially acute for 1960s-era radicals
inspired by Race Pride. One Japanese American commentator explains: "Many of their children do not understand today why the Nisei
G.I.s fought for their oppressors. To the children, the real fighters for

civil rights were the Japanese American dissidents who raised a furor against relocation."[89] The line between patriotism and racial co-optation seems blurry to many Japanese Americans who turned to the relocation resistance to affirm their identities. Thus the identity needs of the Sansei affect the way in which the war is remembered. The descendants' preference for memories of opposition manifests itself not so much in an active downplaying of the role of the G.I.s as in an active highlighting of every conceivable act of resistance.

The most immediate problem for those Japanese Americans who wanted to emphasize resistance to relocation was that there appeared to have been very little. In the camps most of the violence that occurred was "directed not against the authorities but against fellow Japanese Americans who, it was believed, were collaborating with the oppressive government."[90] In the 1970s, though, several authors noticed a form of internment resistance that had not been previously acknowledged: cultural survival.

In a 1973 article in *Amerasia Journal,* Gary Okihiro argued that cultural survival was a form of mass resistance. He concluded that "[b]eyond the visible forms of resistance, between occasional petition, strike or riot, is the true nature of Japanese resistance to white control."[91] The WRA administration failed, Okihiro claimed, "to make them 'assimilable' into white America."[92] The next year, in 1974, two other scholars expressed a similar view of the internment experience: "Through the operation of continuing resistance activity, Manzanar would eventually be transformed into a Little Tokyo of the desert where, as in prewar days, the most salient community characteristics were group solidarity and the predominance of elements of Japanese culture."[93] The fact that Manzanar developed into a productive farm community was now interpreted as an expression of the heroic resilience of Japanese American culture in the face of white oppression: "[T]he entire community served notice that their self-determination and ethnic identity would not be relinquished without a struggle."[94] For activists most concerned to assert a sense of their own ethnic identity, the fact that the camp internees retained their ethnicity was seen as an act of heroic resistance.

The parallel between this interpretation of the camp experience and the Jewish memory of the Holocaust is striking. James E. Young, in a cross-national study of Holocaust memory, argues that "in America's culture of assimilation . . . it is almost always the memory of extreme experience that serves to distinguish the identity of minority groups from the majority population."[95] Young argues that this is true for American Jews, blacks, and Indians. All these groups, he explains, "depend in great measure on the power of a remembered past to bind otherwise alienated groups."[96] To this list Japanese Americans might easily be added, for it is the worst experience of their past that has become the real foundation for their contemporary identity.

Japanese Americans have made similar observations. Reflecting on the fiftieth anniversary of Executive Order 9066 in 1992, Don T. Nakanishi, a Sansei and chairman of UCLA's Asian-American Studies Center, explicitly claimed that Japanese American identity is predicated on a profound awareness of past injustice:

> We must come to see that the unique contribution which we as Japanese Americans can make to American society is not the adding of a so-called "foreign" ingredient to the proverbial melting pot, but instead to share and forever apply our distinct vantage points of this society and of this government, which are based on our unique Internment experience . . . To be a Japanese American, I believe, should mean that the Internment remains at the forefront of our collective memory, and the basis of the most distinct contribution that we can make to society.[97]

It is important to understand that when the past serves as the main, perhaps the only, support for group identity, the events of that past may come to take on even greater significance for later generations than for those who lived through them. One Nisei internee, joking about the younger revisionist historians, touched on this, saying, "If anything, they feel it was a greater wrong than we who were there feel it was."[98]

Conclusions

Japanese American activism first developed in a pan-Asian context. Thus it is important to understand the connections between Asian American Race Pride, Japanese American ethnic identity, and the transformation of American memory. As in the case of the Indians, it was the Race Pride Movement that encouraged pan-Asian identity activism in the late 1960s and early 1970s. Although an enormous influx of immigrants hindered further development of racial consciousness among Asian American ethnic groups, collective memory activism continued to thrive long after the collapse of the pan-Asian activism that sparked it.

The Manzanar case study showed that as Japanese Americans sought to win national recognition of their past, they had to work against the understandable desire of many people to forget any injustice which might muddy the image of the Good War. This struggle against forgetfulness was rather different from that of the Indians, who had to work to convince Americans that they had been wronged in the first place. The traditional vision of the frontier had made the destruction of Indians a feature of national destiny. By contrast, few Americans had ever taken pride in the mass internment of American citizens of Japanese ancestry during World War II. For the most part, then, Japanese Americans had to overcome the inertia of American forgetfulness rather than an ideological justification of the internment.

Such inertia proved strong. Active hostility of residents of Inyo County in the 1970s killed the efforts to gain a California historic site designation for Manzanar. Only good organization and intense lobbying of both local and national politicians by Japanese Americans prevented a similar fate for the national historic site proposal. The public assertion of memory of the World War II internment tragedy now

forms a major foundation for contemporary Japanese American identity.

A striking feature of Japanese American collective memory is its
deeply ethnic character. That is, Japanese Americans remember past
oppression and know that it occurred largely because of their race,
but this awareness has not created a strong sense of solidarity with
other Asian Americans. Patterns of immigration may account for this.
Japanese Americans are now the only Asian American group which is
composed mostly of people born in the United States.[99]

The fact that the majority of Asian Americans today are immigrants is one important reason why a pan-Asian identity has not taken
hold among peoples of Asian ancestry. The fact that the current racial
climate is in many ways better than in the past is perhaps another reason. People with no cultural or coercive incentive to think of themselves as members of a specific group probably will not do so. But because race and ethnic consciousness is produced in a dialectic
between the past and the present, there is no way to predict whether
"Asian American" will continue to refer to a broad range of ethnic
group identities or whether the term will come to signify a shared
community of memory.

CHAPTER THREE

Latinos

A ll of the minority identity affirmations that began in the 1960s were predicated on the common belief that those identities, and the visions of history that supported them, could be changed by direct political action. But sociological realities place distinct limits on the ability of groups to redefine themselves and their histories. Thus, while Indian activism reflects a growing awareness of commonality among the peoples of various tribes, recent Asian immigration has encouraged Asian American identity activism to focus on individual ethnic groups, such as Japanese Americans. The divergent experiences of Indians and Asian Americans illustrate the contingent nature of group identity in America. This contingency is particularly evident in the case of Latinos.

Like all other American minority groups, Latinos have worked since the late 1960s to influence American collective memory. Although Latinos are the second largest minority group in America, their influence has been less than what one might expect from so large a population. That is because Latinos themselves have shown little inclination to represent themselves as a single people with a common history. The reasons for this reluctance will begin to emerge with an overview of the basic characteristics of the Latino population.

Several lines of cleavage cut through the Latino population and prevent the development of a shared identity. The first and most obvious internal division is that of national origin. According to the 1990 Census, 64 percent of Latinos are Mexican Americans (13.3 million people), 10.5 percent are Puerto Ricans, 4.9 percent are Cubans, and another 13.7 percent are from various countries in Central and South America.[1] Latino immigration from all sources except Mexico is almost entirely a late twentieth-century phenomenon. As with Asian Americans, cultural differences deriving from national origin persist among Latino immigrants. These differences are accentuated by the general regional segregation of Latino populations from one another in the United States. Cubans are, for example, heavily concentrated in South Florida, while Puerto Ricans are clustered in New York, and over ninety percent of Mexican Americans live in the Southwest.[2]

Latino groups also differ markedly in their relative status in the general population. While all Puerto Ricans are citizens who can move freely between their homeland and the United States, many Cuban Americans are political refugees. Mexican Americans, in turn, differ from the other Latino groups in that their concentration in the Southwest has substantially defined that region as their own. Sociologist Morris Janowitz has described their unique situation: "[T]he presence of Mexico at the border of the United States, plus the strength of Mexican cultural patterns, means that the 'natural history' of Mexican immigrants has been and will be at variance with that of other immigrant groups. For sections of the Southwest, it is not premature to speak of a cultural and social irredenta—sectors of the United States which have in effect become Mexicanized."[3]

There are other differences among Latinos as well. An obvious one is political affiliation. Puerto Ricans vote largely Democratic, while Cubans are more frequently Republican.[4] Indeed, Cuban immigration has transformed Miami's previously liberal Democratic politics.[5] Another difference among Latinos is race; many Puerto Ricans are black, for example, while few Mexicans are. Moreover, these immigrants come from countries where racial identities are constructed differently than they are in America. Puerto Rican immigrants, for instance, often view race as a gradation from white to black and thus resist the simple dichotomy commonly found in the United States.

Despite the prevalence of the term Latino, most Latinos identify with the culture of their nation of origin or, in the case of most Mexican Americans, their region in the United States. Latinos thus remain Mexican Americans, Puerto Ricans, Cuban Americans, and so on. As with Asian Americans, the persistence of difference is encouraged by America's pluralistic culture. While many Mexican Americans, for example, can recall the ethnic discrimination of the past, millions of recent Mexican immigrants have come into a nation which explicitly protects their rights—in 1975 the protections of the Voting Rights Act were extended to peoples of Spanish heritage, as "language minorities."[6]

In sum, the diversity of the Latino population is so great that it can reasonably be said that there is no such person as a "Latino." In his massive *Latinos: A Biography of the People,* Earl Shorris begins with precisely this assessment: "Although the name of this book is *Latinos,* the theory of it is that there are no Latinos, only diverse people struggling to remain who they are while becoming someone else."[7] Not surprisingly, Latino contributions to American collective memory have been made by distinct ethnic subgroups of the larger Latino population.[8] Thus this case study will take the same form as the previous one, where the contributions of one group (Japanese Americans) were used to illustrate some of the achievements of the larger population (Asian Americans). Because Mexican Americans constitute the largest subset of the Latino population, the remainder of this chapter will focus on them.

Mexican Americans

In *Mexican Americans: The Ambivalent Minority,* political scientist Peter Skerry argues that the most important question facing Mexican Americans today is whether or not to identify themselves as white ethnics or a minority race.[9] That there is a real choice here is apparent from surveys. In the 1990 Census, for example, 51 percent of Mexican Americans identified themselves as white, 1 percent as black, and 48 percent as "Other Race."[10] Interestingly, the percentage of Mexican Americans answering "Other Race" has increased from 45 percent in 1980 to 48 percent in 1990.[11]

This move to racial minority self-identification is, of course, a reflection of changing attitudes among Mexican Americans rather than changing physiognomy. Because the selection of racial identity involves not just skin color but also attitudes about race in general, it is important to understand the cultural influences that now inform Mexican Americans' self-identification. In particular, attitudes about the past shape definitions of present identity. Sociologist Marta Tienda offers this description of Mexican Americans: "[As Mexican Americans] lost their land, their social mobility became blocked, and this eventually led to a deterioration of their social position vis-à-vis Anglos. Racism was employed to pursue economic interests . . . *Although Mexican Americans are white, their brown skin and indigenous features encourage racism and discrimination by the Anglo majority.*"[12] Peter Skerry rightly notes that Tienda's description of Mexican Americans reflects an ambivalence which "typifies the genuine quandary many Mexican Americans face: if they have 'brown skin and indigenous features,' then how can they be characterized as 'white'? And if they are 'white,' then why have they been subjected to 'racism and discrimination'?"[13]

For present purposes, what is most significant about this identity problematic is that those who prefer to see Mexican Americans as white ethnics have created historical narratives which differ markedly from those produced by individuals who choose to see Mexican Americans as racial minorities. What follows is a discussion of the origins and development of both historical visions: an analysis of the attempt to write Mexican American history as that of a white ethnic group, followed by a discussion of the efforts which have been made,

particularly since the 1960s, to construct Mexican American history
as that of a minority race.

The White Ethnic Vision

The origin of the white ethnic vision of Mexican Americans is described at length by Mario García in *Mexican Americans* (1989). García
explains that race took on a new significance in the American Southwest following the Anglo movement into the region after the signing
of the Treaty of Guadalupe Hidalgo in 1848. Anglo settlers often
equated all things Mexican with racial inferiority. García indicates
that many of the long-time inhabitants of the region reacted to Anglo
racism by using "the term 'Spanish' in describing themselves . . .be-
cause they wished to avoid Anglo racism by claiming Spanish lineage
and hence membership in the white race."[14]

This "Spanish" self-definition has persisted and remains particularly
strong among Hispanos, the Mexican Americans of New Mexico. Hispanos respond differently to census questions about ethnic identity
than do Mexican Americans of other states, generally preferring "Spanish American" to "Mexican American."[15] In a book on the Hispano population, Richard Nostrand reaches this conclusion: "[While] Hispanos
reject their Mexican heritage and extol their Spanishness . . . the concept of being Spanish seems not to be a holdover of 'Spaniard' from the
Spanish period, but instead stems from contact with Anglos."[16] Nostrand shows that the nineteenth-century New Mexicans' notion of
being "Spanish" was posed in specific contrast to that of Mexican Americans as a *mestizo* (part Indian) race. Given nineteenth-century American attitudes about Indians, it is not surprising that many Mexican
Americans forcefully asserted their status as whites. Indeed, affirming
"Spanishness" became, after a full century, a tradition itself.[17]

The historical vision associated with Hispano identity is that of the
romantic Old Southwest, a pre-Anglo Spanish halcyon period of

leisure and glory that came and went gracefully. The representation of that vision of history has traditionally been very strong in places like Santa Fe and Taos, New Mexico. The same interpretation also appears in other areas where the Anglo elite either came to control the interpretation of local history or put the Hispanic elite in a position of needing to affirm their European background over their Indian heritage.[18]

For clear historical reasons, then, the Hispanos of New Mexico (and many other Hispanics) emphasized their Spanish identity, sometimes at the expense of more complex historical realities. However, changes in American racial attitudes have mellowed once-aggressive assertions of Spanish heritage. In 1992, for example, Archbishop Robert Sanchez of Santa Fe's St. Francis Cathedral (site of Willa Cather's *Death Comes for the Archbishop*) changed the name of the cathedral's famous Madonna statue from "Our Lady of the Conquest" to the less racially controversial "Our Lady of Peace." The change reflected a growing interest in emphasizing Indian heritage in Santa Fe. Thus the "white Spaniard" vision of the past has been losing its edge in New Mexico as Indian identity has become more valued nationally.[19]

Three additional developments during this century have encouraged Mexican Americans to identify themselves as a racial minority. First, the ideology of the Mexican Revolution of 1910 affirmed the "Indianness" of Mexican identity. Attitudes among twentieth-century immigrants from Mexico and their descendants reflect this change.[20] Second, a growing percentage of Mexican Americans have little or no memory of the racial unrest in the Southwest before the 1960s, specifically of the past stigmatization of peoples of Indian heritage. In fact, self-identification as a racial minority is often perceived to convey, and in some cases does convey, tangible material rewards. Third, Mexican American critics of the white ethnic vision have attempted to assert a positive image of Mexican Americans as nonwhite. As with other expressions of Race Pride, this vision emerged in the political and cultural ferment of the late 1960s.

The Racial Vision: La Raza

Many Mexican Americans participated in the southwestern labor movement of the early and mid-1960s. The grape pickers' strike led by César Chávez in Delano, California, in 1965, announced that change was about to come to the Southwest as it had to the South. This strike, and the decade of conflict that followed, brought Mexican Americans into the mainstream of American political activism. And, just as the Civil Rights Movement laid the groundwork for Black Power, the activism of the United Farm Workers (UFW) and César Chávez encouraged other, often slightly younger, Mexican Americans to reexamine the basic construction of their identity.

Among them was a former boxer, Rodolfo "Corky" Gonzales. In 1967 Gonzales became one of the first to articulate the crisis felt by many young Mexican Americans, in his poem entitled "I Am Joaquín":

> I am Joaquín.
> I am lost in a world of confusion,
> Caught up in the whirl of an Anglo society,
> Confused by the rules,
> Scorned by the attitudes,
> Suppressed by manipulation,
> And destroyed by modern society.[21]
> I am Joaquín
> in a country that has wiped out
> all my history,
> stifled all my pride.[22]

One response to the identity crisis Gonzales described was the development of the term "Chicano" (previously an epithet for lower-class Mexicans) among young Mexican Americans in the late 1960s.[23] Asserting a proud new vision of themselves, young Mexican Americans turned this derogatory term into a symbol of pride.[24] The term gained wide use around the time of the Mexican American boycott of the Los Angeles schools in March of 1968, when some 10,000 students walked out in protest over the poor education they were receiving.[25] One of the students' main complaints was that the schools were presenting negative images of Mexican Americans. The boycott called particular attention to the issue of Mexican American ethnic identity as represented in historical materials.[26]

This desire to change the past reached a new level of articulation at a 1969 meeting in Denver organized by Gonzales's organization, Crusade for Justice. The formal cultural statement emerging from that meeting was called "El plan espiritual de Aztlán." It offered young Mexican Americans a new vision of themselves and their history in the Southwest homeland:

> In the spirit of a new people that is conscious not only of its proud heritage, but also of the brutal "gringo" invasion of our territories, *we,* the Chicano, inhabitants and civilizers of the northern land of Aztlán, from whence came our forefathers, reclaiming the land of their birth and consecrating the determination of our people of the sun, *declare* that the call of our blood is our power, our responsibility, and our inevitable destiny . . . With our heart in our hand and our hands in the soil, we declare the independence of our mestizo Nation. We are a bronze people with a bronze culture. Before the world, before all of North America, before all our brothers in the Bronze Continent, we are a Nation. We are a union of free pueblos. We are *Aztlán.*
>
> To hell with the nothing race.[27]

The rhetoric of Aztlán, first heard in the late 1960s, combined the notion of an alienated homeland (today's southwestern United States) with a conception of Chicanos as a distinct race. The *mestizo* character of the Southwest was aggressively asserted by Chicano activists. In

Chicano Manifesto (1971), Chicago journalist Armando Rendon wrote, "Chicanos have a blood relationship to our Indian forebears. Descendants of early Spanish colonists who reject such an alliance with the Indian natives of the Americas also reject the most obvious claim to the retribution for the misdeeds committed by the Anglos who stole the land."[28] In an early 1970s collection of Chicano literature on the Aztlán concept, the playwright Luis Valdez (who later directed the film *La Bamba*) also connected the Indian heritage vision to assertions of territorial land rights:

> We did not, in fact, come to the United States at all. The United States came to us. We have been in America a long time. Somewhere in the twelfth century, our Aztec ancestors left their homeland in Aztlán, and migrated south to Anáhuac, "the place by the waters," where they built their great city of México-Tenochtilán . . . Aztlán was left far behind, somewhere 'in the north,' but it was never forgotten. Aztlán is now the name of our Mestizo nation, existing north of Mexico, within the borders of the United States.[29]

Given the explicit similarity of their claims, it is not surprising that the Chicano nationalists imitated the Indian Red Power example in both words and deeds. In August 1972, for example, twenty-six Chicano militants from Los Angeles seized Santa Catalina Island and renamed it "Aztlán Libre."[30] Their seizure of the island was inspired by the earlier Indian holdout at Alcatraz (which began in November 1969 and ended in June 1971). The Chicano "reclamation" of Santa Catalina lasted only twenty-four days, but demonstrates the Red Power influence on the Chicano movement. The influence of Black Power was also important: the twenty-six Chicanos at Catalina referred to themselves as Brown Berets and self-consciously modeled their group after the Black Panthers, a radical Black Power group from Oakland.[31] During the early days of the Chicano movement there was even occasional use of the term "Brown Power."[32]

Thus, for a short period in the early 1970s, it seemed that the young Chicano radicals' racial vision of Mexican American identity and heritage might unite Mexican Americans into a new consciousness and then political power. Indeed, the consciousness-raising efforts of Chicano radicals quickly led to the creation in 1970 of a political party, La Raza Unida (The United Race). La Raza was founded by José Angel Gutiérrez and several other student activists at St. Mary's University in San Antonio. After receiving his master's degree from St. Mary's, Gutiérrez returned to Crystal City, in southwestern Texas, where he led a group of La Raza candidates to take control of the City Council in 1970 and the School Board in 1971.[33] Although these victories eventually dissipated because of leadership infighting, the Crystal City successes demonstrated the potential power of Chicano nationalism.

Like many of the early Chicano radicals, Gutiérrez endorsed the idea that Chicanos could be united around a self-consciously created body of racial myths. After the victories in Crystal City, he stated, "[The] Chicano movement has developed much that is indigenous to itself and learned to recast its myths to serve the revolution and define the enemy."[34] Gutiérrez's belief in the efficacy of such myths was further reinforced when, in 1972, La Raza Unida's candidate for Texas governor, Ramsey Muñiz, took 18 percent of the vote in south and west Texas counties and won 6 percent of the vote statewide. Shortly after the election a combination of factors including drug arrests, internal squabbling, and denunciations from traditional Mexican American leaders, such as Texas's Henry Gonzáles, led to La Raza Unida's collapse.[35] In retrospect, 1972 proved to be the highwater mark of Chicano nationalism.

Although La Raza Unida did not develop into a major political party, it raised important questions about the direction that Mexican Americans should take, both culturally and politically. Corky Gonzales's brand of radical Chicano politics put an enormous premium on self-definition. As one commentator put it, Gonzales believed that "the nationalist sense of pride and belief in one's own people ought to over-ride the pragmatism of traditional politics."[36] Gonzales hoped that a radical politics of racial consciousness-raising would encourage local political organization and, in the long run, facilitate massive political change.

Chicano radicalism manifested what Professor Mario Barrera describes as "an almost nostalgic vision of community."[37] The Chicano nationalists wanted a certain skin color to be equated with a way of looking at the world and thus form a common, indissoluble social bond. This utopian cast of Chicano nationalism appeared throughout the early 1970s. Another section from "El plan espiritual de Aztlán" reads: "[Chicano nationalism] transcends all religious, class, political, and economic factions or boundaries. Nationalism is the common denominator that all members of La Raza can agree upon."[38] This dream proved elusive, though. After the mid-1970s Chicano nationalism faded from view, largely relegated to a few universities where it continues to survive in "ethnic studies" departments.[39] Earl Shorris described the state of the Chicano racial dream in the 1990s: "The Chicano generation began in the late 1960s and lasted six or eight years, dying slowly throughout the seventies. Nothing remains of it now but a handshake practiced by middle-aged men. Some people still call themselves Chicanos, but the definition is vague and the word has lost its fire."[40]

What accounts for the decline of the Chicano dream and, more precisely, for the failure of the Aztlán idea to take hold with most Mexican Americans? Some Mexican American scholars have recently suggested that the very concept of Aztlán, the mythical origin of Chicanos, was formulated in such a way as to be unappealing to most Mexican Americans. Daniel Cooper Alarcón, writing in the journal *Aztlán,* stated that "Aztlán increasingly appears to be very much an empty symbol to many Chicanos, a symbol that does not unite so

much as divert those who do not wish to consider the very real differences of religion, gender, class, sexuality, language, and *mestizaje*
within Chicano communities."[41]

This is an important conclusion in that it highlights the difference
between Chicano nationalism and Red Power activism. Whereas the
assertion of a view of Indians as a people with a shared history (rooted
in American oppression) has largely succeeded in American collective
memory, Chicano nationalists were unable to unite Mexican Americans around a single historical vision. Two other students of Chicano
nationalism, Rosa Linda Fregoso and Angie Chabram, develop Alarcón's observations further:

> The shortsightedness of Chicano studies intellectuals was
> that they assumed that the construction of their own self-
> representations as subjects was equivalent to that of the totality
> of the Chicano experience, and that this shared representation
> could be generalized in the interest of the entire group . . .
> How else could we explain the fact that the ahistorical "Aztec"
> identity would fall on the deaf ears of an urban community . . .
> By recuperating the mythic pre-Columbian past and formulat-
> ing this as the basis for our shared identity, Chicano academic
> intellectuals of the post-colonial tradition failed to see that cul-
> tural identities have histories, that they undergo constant trans-
> formation and that far from being etched in the past, cultural
> identities are constantly being constructed.[42]

Perhaps it would be simpler to say that radical Chicano nationalists
overplayed their hand—they had too great a faith in the ability of a
constructed past to unify diverse individuals and interests.[43]

Mario García reaches much the same conclusion: "In its obsession
for a new history and a new culture, the Chicano Generation created
its own myths and 'false consciousness.'"[44] And Bruce-Novoa, writ-

ing in *Aztlán,* observes that the Chicanos had rightly attacked established Anglo myths, but by the very act of challenging one set of myths with another set of myths, they had undermined the possibility of "returning to a belief in a monological history invested with the status of truth."[45] Thus Chicano activists learned that, for Mexican Americans at least, a set of positive myths is not an acceptable substitute for negative myths. The radical Chicano concept of a bronze race descended from the Aztecs seemed to offer an affirmative self-conception for Mexican Americans. Yet Chicano radicalism failed because Mexican Americans themselves did not believe the histories Chicano identity activists (mostly university trained intellectuals) propagated in the 1970s. As many of those intellectuals now recognize, the majority of Mexican Americans were simply uninterested in the vision of themselves as Aztecs.

Neither of the two most fully developed visions of their heritage is now clearly dominant among Mexican Americans. Neither the white ethnic vision nor the myth of Aztlán satisfies Mexican Americans' sense of the complexity of their own identities. Many Mexican Americans believe that the history which portrays them as Spaniards is a racial simplification, and even more doubt the history which portrays them as the descendants of Aztecs. Throughout this work we have seen how changes in group identity, sparked by Race Pride, fueled efforts to change American memory. On the whole, the causal explanation has been straightforward: changes in group identification (increased pride) led to mobilization to change the national memory. But because there is no viable unifying historical narrative for Mexican Americans, this pattern does not obtain here. While Race Pride has encouraged Mexican American efforts to reform national memory, continuing ambivalence and disagreements about how to characterize their contemporary identity have made it difficult for them to forcefully assert a vision of the past. This truth is best illustrated by an examination of the Mexican American efforts to change the interpre-

tation of the past presented at the most famous of all southwestern
history sites, the Alamo.

Remembering the Alamo

The defense of the Alamo in San Antonio against the forces of Mexican General Santa Anna in 1836 is certainly one of most famous
events in American history. It gave rise to heroic images of Captain
Travis, Jim Bowie, and their volunteer force fighting to the last man
against a much larger Mexican army. But the siege of the Alamo was
only one fight in the Texas War for Independence, which had begun
five months earlier at the Battle of Gonzales and which ended two
months after the Alamo fell with the crushing defeat of Santa Anna at
San Jacinto. These seven months of 1835–36 constitute the Southwest's Revolutionary War. As in the Revolutionary War in the East
sixty years earlier, the fight began as an assertion of territorial rights
by colonists and eventually became a struggle for independence.

While the people and events of both wars were heavily mytholo-
gized by later generations, there is one major difference in the memory of the two wars. The Revolutionary War in the East was remembered by later generations as a contest between two peoples of
similar racial stock—that is, as a purely political struggle. In contrast,
American memory of the Alamo has traditionally pitted Alamo defenders, who were believed to be all white, against Mexicans, who
were characterized as foreign browns. The historian Paul Andrew
Hutton rightly observes that a "creation myth does not pander to liberal sensibilities. The lines of good and evil are always razor sharp.
The story is meant to give to a people a strong and unique self-image.
It does not cater to the enemy in any way. Thus the myth of the
Alamo is often stunningly racist."[46] The Alamo has become a symbol
of racism to many people, not so much for what happened in 1836, as
for how later generations of Anglos who controlled the site chose to
remember the conflict.

The defense of the Alamo took place in 1836, but it was only during the heightened nationalism of the late nineteenth century that Americans began to take an active interest in preserving the battle site and interpreting it for future generations.[47] The buildings most people visit in San Antonio today became Texas state property in 1905. At that time the state granted the right of care for and interpretation of the Alamo to an organization that had been active in the preservation of the site for more than a decade, the Daughters of the Republic of Texas (DRT).[48] Founded in 1891, the DRT is a genealogical society that has maintained tight control of the interpretation of the Alamo to this day. The Alamo is thus unusual for a national historic site in that it is state-owned but is run and interpreted by a private organization.

Although dedicated to promoting the preservation and representation of all Texas heritage, the DRT's membership is determined strictly by genealogy: "Any woman wishing to be a Daughter must be . . . able to trace ancestors to the early Anglo colonists of the 1820s or prove that her ancestors in Texas 'aided in establishing the independence of Texas or served the Republic of Texas in maintaining its independence' prior to its annexation to the United States in 1846.'"[49] Thus all descendants of the Anglo settlers, whether they fought for the cause or not, are eligible for membership, while only descendants of those Mexican Americans who can prove active assistance to the cause of independence qualify. Not surprisingly, the Daughters are nearly all Anglos.

The history that the DRT has traditionally presented has downplayed the fact that the Alamo was the Mission San Antonio de Valero for two hundred and fifty years before 1836. All of the Alamo defenders that the DRT has chosen to glorify by name were Anglos. Few today remember the names of any of the Mexicans who died inside the Alamo. And despite clear evidence that many Alamo defenders were fighting to secure their constitutional rights as Mexican citizens, the Daughters have interpreted the battle in light of the later

achievement of Texas independence. The effect has been to simplify
the tensions at work in Texas history.

The message that the Alamo is an Anglo history site is reinforced
by the types of activities the DRT allows at the site. In particular, the
DRT permits only two other groups to make use of the Alamo, the
San Antonio Cavaliers and the Order of the Alamo. The Cavaliers are
an elite, all-Anglo group which meets annually to elect one of its
members "King Antonio" for the Fiesta San Antonio, the city's major
self-celebration.[50] The Cavaliers are a spin-off of an earlier organization, the Order of the Alamo, which was founded in 1909. The
Order remains active, with much membership overlap with the Cavaliers, and elects the "Queen Angelina" for the Fiesta, always a daughter of one of the men of the Order.[51]

The DRT's monopolization of the Alamo sends a powerful message to the city's non-Anglo residents. The resultant tensions can be
seen in the celebrations that have revolved around the Alamo. The Fiesta de San Antonio is held annually during the week of April 21, the
anniversary of the victory of Sam Houston's forces over Santa Anna.
The Fiesta began as a tourist attraction in the 1890s, but has always
been an occasion for symbolic enactment of civic power. From 1913
until the late 1940s the Fiesta was actually known as Fiesta San Jacinto.[52] Although San Jacinto was a glorious victory for the Texans, it
can also be viewed as a massacre of Mexican troops (9 Anglo and 600
Mexican dead). The celebration of that event thus had a racial tinge
that kept local Mexican Americans away for decades. Only when the
festival name was changed to Fiesta de San Antonio, suggesting inclusion of the whole city, did Hispanic groups become involved.

In 1947 the League of United Latin American Citizens (LULAC)
began electing its own alternative King for the Fiesta, the Rey Feo.[53]
Each year the Rey Feo is the man who raises the most money for
LULAC's scholarship fund. Although the Rey Feo and King Antonio
now open the Fiesta together in front of the Alamo, they represent
two very different heritage camps. That their symbolic point of con-

tention continues to be the Alamo is clear from the fact that while King Antonio is invited to the crowning of the Rey Feo at San Fernando Cathedral each year, the Rey Feo is not allowed to witness the crowning of King Antonio inside the Alamo.

Mexican Americans and the Alamo

Since the mid-1960s affirmations of race and ethnic group pride have radically altered American memory. Recent events in San Antonio suggest that a major change is about to occur at the Alamo as well. However, given that the Race Pride Movement began over twenty-five years ago, it is first necessary to explain why change is coming so late in San Antonio.

One reason for the durability of Anglo control is institutional. As described earlier, the Alamo is unusual among major American history sites in that, while state-owned, it is controlled by a private genealogical society. The DRT's traditional role as guardian of the site has yielded an interpretation even more resistant to Race Pride than that found at the old Custer Battlefield, where a group of military historians were able to forestall change for a decade after Indian protests began. The DRT's control of the Alamo is total. The Daughters maintain an armed private security force at the site and allow no on-site protests. While Indians were able to protest the Custer interpretation from the first flourishing of Red Power, the Alamo has never experienced a major protest inside its walls.[54]

The second reason for the continuity of Alamo interpretation has to do with the general political climate of San Antonio. While Los Angeles was torn apart by Chicano-Anglo conflicts in the 1960s, San Antonio remained calm.[55] Although Chicano radicalism developed in San Antonio in the 1960s and 1970s, it has had less influence there than in Los Angeles or even other parts of Texas where the Mexican immigrant population is greater. In fact, San Antonio has received relatively small numbers of immigrants from Mexico in modern times. While 46 percent of Mexican Americans living in metropolitan Los Angeles in 1980 were foreign-born, in San Antonio the number was only 12 percent.[56]

Another moderating influence, beyond the lack of immigration, is that Mexican Americans constitute 56 percent of the population of San Antonio and have never been excluded from the franchise. They are culturally separate from the Anglo elite but at the same time constitute a powerful force in politics. In San Antonio, unlike in Los Angeles, Mexican Americans are well represented in government.[57] Numerous nationally prominent politicians come from the area: Henry Gonzáles, Albert Peña, Henry Cisneros, and others.

Despite this political integration, San Antonio has long been marked by Anglo-Hispanic tension, manifested in, among other things, sharp residential segregation. Most Anglos live on the North Side, while Mexican Americans live on the West and South Sides, leaving the black population to the East. Not surprisingly, money is also a major source of contention. The average income for Mexican Americans is little more than half that of San Antonio Anglos.[58]

Although San Antonio lacks a manufacturing base, there are enough opportunities that Mexican Americans are not forced to unite around purely ethnic politics. Preoccupation with economic mobility rather than the symbols of identity has long marked the San Antonio Hispanic community, known for the saying "Forget the Alamo!" Establishment of the Rey Feo in 1947 signaled the emergence of a distinct Hispanic middle class. Gilberto Hinojosa, professor at Incarnate Word College in San Antonio, describes the mood of the time: "There was definitely a 'we have arrived' kind of thing that prevented any kind of single-action demonstration [against the symbolism of the Alamo]."[59] Economic opportunities and political integration have thus discouraged purely ethnic politics.

As important as these factors are in explaining the stability of Alamo interpretation, it is the sheer complexity of Tejano (Mexican Americans of Texas) identity which constitutes the greatest barrier to single-issue activism within the community. Although American culture encourages Mexican Americans to define themselves as white ethnics or minorities, Mexican Americans in San Antonio experience an ambivalence about this division which has made it difficult for them to unite against Anglo assertions of heritage at the Alamo. Hinojosa describes the identity experience of many San Antonians:

> It's ambivalence in a number of ways. First, Mexican Americans do not have a clear race view of themselves. The reason is the mixture of races is so profound and so thorough that it is very difficult to clearly designate, you know Spanish, Mexican, Indian features. You can tell extremes but there's this whole group in the middle that is hard to pinpoint. Even within my own family, I'd like to point out, one of my daughters is lighter than I am. The other is darker. So the race thing is difficult to pinpoint.
>
> Second, immigration from Mexico has continued and thus Mexican Americans find themselves at different stages of acculturation and assimilation. So the ambiguity of race plus the ambiguity of assimilation and acculturation make it difficult for Mexican Americans to form a clear sense of who they are either racially or ethnically.[60]

This ambivalence about race and ethnic heritage is a common feature of local Mexican American organizations, even those devoted to promoting a specific conception of their heritage. Take, for example, the Granaderos de Galvez, a Spanish-heritage organization in San Antonio. Its president, Robert Benavides, is also past president of the Canary Islanders Descendants Association, a genealogical group that traces its ancestry to the founding Spanish elite of San Antonio. Despite his strong emphasis on Spanish heritage, Benavides displays a reluctance to embrace a simple white ethnic view of his own past:

You have those who trace [their ancestry] back to clearly Spanish colonizers . . . naturally they are going to relate to the white
ethnic identification. But they also have to relate, if they have
any intermarriage with anybody from Mexico, to being a Mexican. Now when you go into the Mexican situation, it's a matter
of, well, was he a Creole Mexican or was he a mestizo, was he
half Indian and then all the variations on that, maybe even
black.

Attitudes about this stuff change. The identification with the Indian [among local Hispanics] is probably the most recent of all
sociological events. To be proud of your Indian heritage is now
fine, just like I'm proud of my particular one.[61]

One might expect the Canary Islanders Association in San Antonio to
manifest an aggressive racial posture. Yet even Benavides, the organization's past president, maintains a willingness to expand the white
ethnic narrative. "There are people who overplay the Canary Islander
thing. But there is a lot of choice here. Now, when do you stop being
white and become something else?" Benavides acknowledges that he
could identify with his Indian ancestry, but opts to identify himself as
a white ethnic. He emphasizes choice.

Resistance to the simplistic white/nonwhite dichotomy is also
found among many of those San Antonians who choose to identify
themselves as Indians. For example, Gary Gabehart, President of the
Inter-Tribal Council of Texas and an enrolled Chickasaw Indian, describes his connection to the Canary Islanders Descendants Association: "There is a Spanish heritage group here, the Canary Islanders
Descendants Association. These guys are really into being Spanish.
You know my brother is head of that group now."[62] Gabehart expresses a certain nonchalance about his identification with the Indian
side of his ancestry, but he takes care to differentiate himself from
those who believe there is a single cultural essence to Indian identity.
"My group are essentially urban Indians. And we are not into the

pow-wow road wooly boogerism and New Age stuff you often see these days."[63]

Further identity confusion in San Antonio comes from the relatively small post-1910 Mexican immigrant population. Mexican Americans who have migrated since the 1910 Revolution tend to emphasize the Indian side of their heritage a little more strongly, reflecting changing ideology in Mexico itself.[64]

The complexity of Tejano race/ethnic identity thus explains the inability or reluctance of local residents to engage the Anglo elite directly on the issue of heritage. While unhappy with the exclusion of all things non-Anglo, the local Mexican American population has been divided on what, in fact, the alternative should be. This division was particularly noticeable in the varied reactions to the opening of the IMAX film *Alamo . . . The Price of Freedom* in a permanent theater across the street from the Alamo in 1988.

The IMAX film company produces special giant-screen movie productions about natural and historic sites around America. At the Grand Canyon, for example, one can avoid the effort of going into the Canyon itself by watching the IMAX film of the Canyon in an air-conditioned theater. In 1988 IMAX opened a theater across the street from the Alamo and began showing a 45-minute film that centered on Colonel William Travis, the commanding officer of the defending forces during the siege. The producers of the film sought to avoid any potential conflict by bringing several local Tejanos into the production process. Robert Benavides, who was part of an advisory committee for the film, explained that the Hispanic viewers had about a dozen problems with an early version of the film, most of which the producer corrected.

Difficulties with the film remained. For example, although scholarly opinion has it that the Alamo defenders likely fought under a Mexican flag with 1824 (the year of the Mexican Constitution) painted on it, the producers intentionally created a new flag in order to downplay the defenders' connection to Mexico.[65] Moreover, the film concluded with a silhouetted image of Mexican soldiers mutilating Jim Bowie. This final image, and the film's negligible coverage of Tejano defenders, triggered the first major local protest at the Alamo, a protest which illuminated the divisions among local Mexican Americans.

At the theater's opening, held on the 152nd anniversary of the fall of the Alamo, about seventy-five local Hispanics protested the film and called for a boycott of the organization that underwrote the cost of production. Professor Hinojosa wrote a statement which protesters handed out at the premiere. In it he lamented that "viewers will get the same message they received from previous versions of the Alamo story: Mexican Americans, the cultural descendants of those Tejanos, are not full members of our society."[66] In an interview Hinojosa explained how the protest also mirrored the divergent conceptions of identity among local Mexican Americans: "You had this situation where you had Mexican Americans being consultants for the IMAX film, Mexican Americans doing the protest, and Mexican Americans crossing the line to go in and see the film. Again, this is a good example of the local ambivalence about how to define the Hispanic identity."[67]

Robert Benavides chose to attend the premiere despite misgivings about the film. He later explained his ambivalence about the event: "I was approached by a group of 90 percent Hispanic protesters. I said, 'You guys write down the name of the Tejanos, the native Mexicans that died in the Alamo, then I'll join you. Until then how the hell can you claim that this movie does not represent the truth.' Of course, the movie had all kinds of problems, but the protesters outside were just about as ill-informed as the people inside."[68]

The divisions within the Hispanic community made manifest during the film protest also suggest that it is unlikely that a Hispanic equivalent of Davy Crockett, Jim Bowie, or William Travis will ever emerge. Reflecting on how those heroes became prominent during the nationalist period of 1890–1910, Professor Hinojosa said, "I am

not sure modern society can do that for any person Hispanic or otherwise."[69]

The IMAX film turned out to be a beginning, not so much of Hispanic unity, but of opposition to the total control of the Alamo by the
Daughters of the Republic of Texas. Enough local Hispanics were
provoked by the DRT's endorsement of the *Price of Freedom* to publicly question their right to control what is, after all, a state-owned
historic site. Members of the League of United Latin American Citizens even suggested that they take administrative control of the
Alamo for a period. Their proposal was quietly dropped, but questions continued to be asked about the DRT's monopoly.[70]

Initially it appeared that the only way to challenge the DRT's control of the Alamo would be to pass legislation repealing the agreement the state had signed with the DRT in 1905. The first action toward this end was a failure. The year after the IMAX opening, a state
representative from Houston, Ron Wilson, proposed a bill in the
Texas State Legislature to put the Alamo under the direct control of
the Parks and Wildlife Department, which runs all other state-owned
historic sites. The bill was easily defeated. Looking back on the
episode, Wilson reflected on the quixotic idea of taking the Daughters out of the Alamo: "They exercise tremendous political clout out
here [in Austin]. They're definitely a formidable opponent. I have the
highest regard for them . . . [T]hey literally kicked my butt."[71] Wilson's failure confirmed, for anyone who was in doubt, that the Anglo
elite had firm control of the site. Opponents of the DRT continued to
look for a way to crack that control. Ironically, the opening turned
out to be in front of the Alamo itself.

The Alamo that most Americans know today was only a small part
of the larger Mission San Antonio de Valero that originally extended
out into the area in front of the compound now run by the DRT.
Most of the outer walls of the compound that visitors now see at the
Alamo were put up in the 1930s by the Works Progress Administration (WPA). In addition, restaurants and shops now line a street

which passes over the site of one of the Alamo's original walls. These changes obscure the fact that the Alamo compound originally extended well into the plaza in front of the current structure.

During the Spanish period, the Mission was a center of activity, and many of the community members were buried nearby. Most of these residents were Indians, a point that took on particular importance in 1994. Early in that year, the Intertribal Council of American Indians announced that they believed Indians were buried near the site of an old wall which is now under the street in front of the DRT's compound. These remains, Intertribal Council Chairman Gary Gabehart claimed, were subject to a new federal law, the Native American Graves Protection and Repatriation Act (NAGPRA).[72] (The wide-ranging power NAGPRA gives Indians is described in Chapter 1.) With this legislation behind them, the small Intertribal Council was able to shut down all traffic on the street that passes in front of the Alamo. Gabehart commented on both the graves and the past problems of Hispanics with the DRT: "I think we've got troubled ground. We've had cars, buses and horses running over that cemetery for years. And what goes around, comes around."[73]

Interestingly, the information which enabled Gabehart to bring about the traffic shutdown around the Alamo came from John Leal, a local Hispanic scholar who wanted to see Spanish heritage better represented in the area. In 1988 he had expressed his unhappiness with the DRT to a researcher: "They're trying to erase us, and we refuse to be erased."[74] Leal translated a series of colonial burial records and discovered evidence that suggested the location of Indian graves. Under NAGPRA, evidence of a grave site provided all those opposed to the DRT with leverage over the Alamo Plaza area. Thus it became unnecessary for locals with very different views of themselves to unite around a single vision of the past.[75] Those Tejanos who emphasized their Spanish heritage and those who emphasized their Indian heritage could avail themselves of a legal measure which expanded

the physical space, and thus the interpretation of the Alamo, to include both Indians and Spaniards.

The San Antonio City Council responded to the crisis by establishing the Alamo Plaza Study Committee in March 1994. The Committee's stated purpose was to "determine the best way to design the
closing of Alamo Plaza East on a permanent basis."[76] The Plaza Committee met regularly from March to October and included representatives from all groups with an interest in the interpretation of the
Alamo, from Indians to blacks to Anglos. It was, in fact, the first time
in San Antonio history that every faction with an interest in interpreting the Alamo had sat down to discuss the past. Some participants
were no doubt eager to challenge the Daughters' of the Republic of
Texas control of their land, but Committee Co-Chairmen Howard
Peak and Roger Perez kept the proceedings focused on the restoration of the original plaza of the Mission San Antonio de Valero.

Several members of the Committee commented that the discussion of interpretation worked well because it was understood that
there would be more space than just the DRT's present site. Peak,
for example, stressed that he made a conscious effort to keep discussion away from the DRT's historic control of the "Alamo" compound: "We really would have started having trouble with the Committee if we had gotten into the management aspects of the Alamo.
And that's why I was very clear and had to remind folks from time to
time that we were talking about Alamo Plaza."[77] The Committee's
final report, issued in October 1994, calls for the inclusion of several
interpretive themes in the expanded Alamo Plaza, including "the
story of the environment and the Native Americans," the area's Spanish heritage, the battle of 1836, and the modern development of San
Antonio.[78]

At this writing, the city is just beginning the process of calling for
design proposals, some of which will suggest moving buildings in
order to expand the plaza. Several Mexican American Committee

members expressed optimism about expanding the interpretation of the past in the near future. Gilberto Hinojosa, for example, explained that "We have to move the battle outside of the present Alamo complex. And if the story is told outside then the Daughters are not the only ones who can tell it . . . They are now fighting even the closing of the street. They are threatening to sue the city for violation of the 1974 or 1976 [sic, actually 1975] agreement with the DRT to leave those streets open. Because even the possibility that the streets would be closed would bring the possibility that the battle would come outside. . . . My purpose is to chip away at that."[79] Robert Benavides echoed these sentiments. "I found if you're going to be successful [in changing interpretation], don't talk about history. Talk about legalities of how the site runs."[80] Thinking back on the advances of the last year, Gary Gabehart of the Inter-Tribal Council also affirmed that "If we had been the kind of people who hold protests and make a lot of noise, nothing would ever have gotten done."[81]

Unable to unite around a single vision of themselves and their history, Mexican Americans in San Antonio have been able to undermine Anglo interpretive hegemony of the Alamo through a legal assault on the land around the area controlled by the Daughters of the Republic of Texas. Thus it appears that in the near future the Alamo will look much more like the rest of San Antonio: historically and racially diverse.

Conclusions

Uniform visions of the past can be successfully asserted only by groups which are culturally and politically united in the present. Latinos, like Asian Americans, tend not to think of themselves as a people with a common historical experience. As a result, they have not exerted a unified impact on American collective memory.

The experiences of one Latino group, Mexican Americans, also illustrate this theme of disunity. While negative stereotyping of Mexican Americans has declined as American racial attitudes have changed, no new history, and certainly no vivifying images of Mexican Americans, have gained wide currency. The attempts of Chicano radicals to create positive myths fizzled out in the 1970s. Chicano nationalism failed to create a sense of racial solidarity among Mexican Americans, because, like the white ethnic identification, it did not adequately capture the complexity of Mexican American identity. Mexican Americans are therefore unusual in that they do not share a clearly dominant vision of their heritage.[82]

This is well illustrated by the experience of Mexican Americans in San Antonio, where their divergent views about heritage and identity have made it difficult for them to successfully oppose Anglo control of the Alamo. The limited success they have enjoyed has not been the result of concerted action, but of the physical expansion of the Alamo itself, making space available for multiple histories. Thus Mexican Americans were able to change the interpretation of the Alamo without agreeing upon a single vision of their past.

The Alamo case illustrates an interesting point about the Race Pride Movement: its strongest expressions have come from those populations most consistently forced to think of themselves as a coherent group. Because they have endured consistent historical oppression and lacked new immigration, Indians have been able to transcend their tribal differences and assert a successful pan-tribal (racial) vision. Conversely, because of less consistent historical oppression and much new immigration, Asian Americans and Mexicans Americans (and other Latinos) have not been able to unite around a vision of their contemporary identity or heritage.

CHAPTER FOUR

Blacks

The Race Pride Movement attempted to bring minorities into the cultural mainstream by asserting the worth of their heritages. Black Power was the first expression of this movement and its most powerful. Beginning in the mid-1960s, Black Power advocates signaled that the new frontier in the struggle for minority equality would be American culture, particularly American collective memory. Although each minority group which followed their lead in the 1960s was faced with challenges unique to its situation, all were inspired by the strong assertions of identity and heritage by black Americans.

Just as black Americans desired full citizenship in America long before the Civil Rights Movement, they also desired cultural recognition long before Black Power. While their struggles to achieve political power in America are commonly remembered today, similar efforts to change American culture are often forgotten. For black activists, though, the connection between power and culture was obvious. After all, the laws which constituted the Jim Crow system were rooted in cultural beliefs about the inferiority of blacks. Recognizing this, opponents of white dominance fought both a legal and a cultural battle for equality. And during the nearly century-long battle against segregation prior to the 1960s, black cultural resistance often involved resisting the white vision of the past. To understand why the Race Pride Movement began with blacks, it is important, then, to review these early expressions of the Race Pride dream.

A Century of Opposition

After the Civil War America was legally a unified nation, but it was not clear what shared memories its citizens would embrace.[1] The common national memories that developed after the war showed the strain of reconciling two peoples—Southerners and Yankees—to a single society. This tension was most evident in the national memory of race. In the years after the Compromise of 1877 ended Reconstruction, public recollection of slavery and its injustices took a strange turn. As numerous historians have shown, the southern interpretation of slavery, the War, and Reconstruction eventually gained acceptance north of the Mason-Dixon line.[2] In a reversal of the rule that the victors write the history, the South's interpretation of the ante-bellum and Civil War past became dominant in the restored nation. Eventually, a highly romanticized vision of the plantation South became common among both northern and southern whites, displacing memories of the injustice of slavery and of the valiant work of abolitionists. (The film *Gone with the Wind* is a familiar expression of the historical vision that became dominant in American—that is, nonblack—memory.) Understandably, black Americans witnessed the development of this vision of the past with disbelief and fear.

Frederick Douglass, for example, wrote in vigorous opposition to a trend he was powerless to stop. Decrying the national rhetoric of reconciliation, predicated as it was on ignoring the past and present mistreatment of blacks in the South, Douglass declared: "Now citizens: I am not indifferent to the claims of a generous forgetfulness, but whatever else I may forget, I shall never forget the difference between those who fought for liberty and those who fought for slavery."[3] As national memory of the injustice of slavery slipped away and the compromises which made Jim Crow possible matured, Douglass found his memory ever more at odds with that of the white-majority nation. Southern whites willfully forgot their past, and northern whites showed little commitment to abolitionist history. Douglass saw that memories of slavery would have to be preserved by blacks. In 1888, despairing of the nation's collective amnesia, he declared, "Well the nation may forget, it may shut its eyes to the past, and frown upon any who may do otherwise, but the colored people of this country are bound to keep the past in lively memory till justice shall be done them."[4]

Increasingly, remembrance of America's abolitionist past and the horrors of slavery was limited to black communities, which preserved those memories in the Jubilee celebrations that commemorated Emancipation.[5] The segregation that developed in the late nineteenth century was thus not simply physical, it was also cultural. America was divided into two different communities of memory. Blacks held on to their memories of past injustices and triumphs, while whites embraced a vision which flattered whites, partly by excluding consideration of the black experience.

Like the physical segregation of the races, a segregation of memory developed during the period of intense racial violence that lasted from 1889 to 1915.[6] It was during this time that white supremacist Thomas Dixon's infamous novels, including *The Leopard's Spots* and *The Clansman,* sold widely. In 1915 D. W. Griffith remade *The Clansman* into the film *The Birth of a Nation.* After a private showing of Griffith's film, which presented Klansmen as heroes, President Woodrow Wilson said the movie "was like writing history with lightning."[7] The President could just as easily have said "writing history with lynching," for Griffith's vision of the past was paralleled by hundreds of local acts of violence against blacks. Brutally suppressed in the present, blacks were in no position to debate the past. Intense white violence thus created an America in which the races led separate lives and remembered separate histories.

Because America segregated into two different communities of memory, it is tempting to ask what effect white memory, supported by violence, had on black memory and identity. This is an obvious but incomplete question, because historically blacks and whites have dialectically shaped both American culture and each other, even during segregation. Thus any discussion of the effects of white hegemony on black identity and memory must also address the awful toll that this suppression took on white identity and memory. While blacks suffered horribly from oppression, whites were made lesser people for inflicting that damage. In *The Mind of the South,* W. J. Cash observed that "Negro entered into white man as profoundly as white man entered into Negro—subtly influencing every gesture, every word, every emotion and idea, every attitude."[8] As the following discussion shows, blacks and whites made and remade each other in their terrible dialogue.

Frederick Douglass once observed that "[t]he past is . . . the mirror in which we may discern the dim outlines of the future."[9] His fear that a false past would legitimate an unjust future motivated him to fight a losing battle against the romantic image of the slave South, an image which would discourage blacks from thinking about the past for generations to come. Historian Carter Woodson commented at the founding of Negro History Week (which later became Black History Month) in 1926: "The Negro knows practically nothing of his history and his 'friends' are not permitting him to learn it . . . And if a race has no history, if it has no worth-while tradition, it becomes a negligible factor in the thought of the world, and it stands in danger of extermination."[10] By Woodson's time living memory of slavery and the Civil War had grown so dim that he was afraid that white-dominated national memory might overwhelm black attempts to promote their alternative collective memory of slavery.

There was, of course, no real possibility that blacks would forget that their ancestors had been slaves. But white images of ante-bellum bliss and the constant threat of physical attack undeniably discouraged the serious study of the past. Forgetfulness, as Carter Woodson warned, became a real danger.

An important indicator of the underdeveloped state of black collective memory in the generations before the 1960s is that not a single major museum of black history was created before the 1960s, while scores were created for white history.[11] Perhaps the largest and most extreme expression of the white ability to define the past was Colonial Williamsburg in Virginia, restoration of which began in the late 1920s. Williamsburg presented an image of the colonial South from which the injustices of slavery were decidedly absent.[12]

One might have hoped that the professionalization of American history which began in the universities at the turn of the century would have resulted in a more serious examination of black history. It did not. W. E. B. Du Bois, himself a member of the first generation of university-trained American historians, thought the professional historical treatment of black American history was so poor that he divided the bibliography of his *Black Reconstruction* (1935) into works in which the author "believe[s] the Negro to be sub-human and congenitally unfitted for citizenship and the suffrage" and works which "write sympathetically about them," the latter category containing substantially fewer entries.[13] Du Bois felt that professionalism had done little to alter the national (nonblack) perception of black history, and of slavery in particular. In the final chapter of *Black Reconstruction,* titled "The Propaganda of History," he even suggested that the professional historians had worked to take the edge off the raw injustice of slavery:

> Our histories tend to discuss American slavery so impartially, that in the end nobody seems to have done wrong and everybody was right. Slavery appears to have been thrust upon unwilling helpless America, while the South was blameless in becoming its center. The difference of development, North and South, is explained as a sort of working out of cosmic social and economic order.[14]

> This is education in the Nineteen Hundred and Thirty-fifth year of the Christ; this is modern and exact social science; this is the university course in "History 12."[15]

When Du Bois wrote this, the year before Margaret Mitchell published *Gone with the Wind,* it appeared that Frederick Douglass's worst
fears had been realized. Douglass had warned against "overgenerous
forgetfulness" among whites, and in 1935 Du Bois had to affirm, "We
fell under the leadership of those who would compromise with the
truth in the past in order to make peace in the present and guide policy
in the future."[16] Like Frederick Douglass decades earlier, Du Bois believed that reconciliation between the North and the South had been
predicated on forgetting black history: "We have been cajoling and flat-
tering the South and slurring the North, because the South is determined to re-write the history of slavery and the North is not interested
in history but in wealth."[17] He added that, beyond money, there was
deeper common motive: "[T]he facts of American history have in the
last half century been falsified because the nation was ashamed. The
South was ashamed because it fought to perpetuate human slavery. The
North was ashamed because it had to call in the black men to save
the Union, abolish slavery and establish democracy."[18]

In addition to documenting American forgetfulness, Du Bois also
described the impact of false American memory on black consciousness and identity. In *The Souls of Black Folk* (1903) he wrote that "the
Negro is a sort of seventh son, born with a veil, and gifted with second
sight in this American world—a world which yields him no true self-
consciousness, but only lets him see himself through the revelation of
the other world. It is a peculiar sensation, this double-consciousness,
this sense of always looking at one's self through the eyes of others."[19]
Much intellectual energy has been spent analyzing this famous passage,
but it seems, in the context of Du Bois's career as a historian, to refer in
part to the constant battle in black American consciousness to be true
to memories that hegemonic forces were attempting to destroy. Thus
blacks developed Du Bois's "second sight"—critical insight into America's hypocritical self-conception, a self-conception supported by false
memories. Although rarely discussed this way, "double consciousness"
is inextricably linked to the problem of American memory. And be-

cause of this "second sight," most of the best American writing on the connections between collective memory, identity, and power is found in the work of black authors.

The notion that America as a whole paid a high price for her forgetfulness has been expressed by many black intellectuals. In 1941, toward the end of *12 Million Black Voices,* Richard Wright said that the story of black suffering was the story of the sorrow of the entire nation and that the recovery of that memory was necessary to restore the integrity of the nation in the present: "We black folk, our history and our present being, are a mirror of all the manifold experiences of America. What we want, what we represent, what we endure is what America *is.* If we black folk perish, America will perish. If America has forgotten her past, then let her look into the mirror of our consciousness and she will see the *living* past living in the present."[20] Wright saw that the problem of black memory was fundamentally a problem of American memory, that the lie which suppressed black memory also gave dominant national (white) memory an unreal quality which was pernicious to the majority as well as to the minority. To maintain a lie entails psychic costs, certainly not so great as that of living beneath the lie, but real costs nonetheless.

A generation after Richard Wright, James Baldwin eloquently described both halves of this dialectic in *The Fire Next Time* (1963). In the letter to his nephew which prefaces the work, Baldwin expresses his version of "double consciousness." He warns his nephew to beware of the debilitating effects of white national memory: "The details and symbols of your life have been deliberately constructed to make you believe what white people say about you."[21] Baldwin also describes the minds of whites: "They are, in effect, still trapped in a history which they do not understand; and until they understand it, they cannot be released from it. They have had to believe for many years, and for innumerable reasons, that black men are inferior to white men."[22] Later Baldwin says that blacks have tried "insofar as this was possible, to dismiss white people as the slightly mad victims of their own brain-washing."[23]

The black radicals who came of age in the 1960s also thought deeply about the relationship between their actions and white consciousness. Even Malcolm X, a black separatist for most of his political career, reflected on the benefits of the liberation of black memory for whites: "I'll tell you something. The whole stream of Western philosophy has now wound up in a cul-de-sac. The white man has perpetrated upon himself, as well as upon the black man, so gigantic a fraud that he has put himself into a crack. He did it through his elaborate, neurotic necessity to hide the black man's true role in history."[24] Malcolm X's words express a common understanding of the connection that existed between white power/identity and black powerlessness/identity, a connection largely forgotten by whites and blacks who have come of age since the 1960s.

The problem of American collective memory appears in the writings of virtually every major black intellectual before 1970. In the decades between *Black Reconstruction* and the rise of the Black Power movement in the 1960s, reshaping the past was always front and center among black thinkers. Even the most familiar figures of the Civil Rights movement were concerned about memory and black self-esteem. Martin Luther King, Jr., for example, explicitly discussed the effects of white memory on blacks: "The history books, which have almost completely ignored the contribution of the Negro in American History, have only served to intensify the Negro's sense of worthlessness and to augment the anachronistic doctrine of white supremacy."[25] A generation before King, Arthur A. Schomburg, in "The Negro Digs Up His Past," argued that "[t]he American Negro must remake his past in order to make his future."[26] The breakthroughs of the Civil Rights Movement in the mid-1960s proved that it was possible for blacks to make their future. Inspired by the accomplishments of Civil Rights, a slightly younger generation of black intellectuals moved quickly to remake their past. Their efforts marked the beginning of the Race Pride Movement.

Black Power

Black Power is a term which still evokes instant recognition and emotion, though often confusedly. Some remember little more than that Stokely Carmichael shouted those words at a Mississippi rally in 1966. Others remember Black Power in some vague association with SNCC (Student Nonviolent Coordinating Committee), the Black Panthers, or the riots of the late 1960s. Still others equate the term with Malcolm X and black separatism. As one attempts to look back through the fire and smoke that engulfed America in the late 1960s, it is easy to lose sight of the issues that Black Power addressed.

In its many incarnations, Black Power dealt with the limitations blacks still faced after the legal breakthroughs of the mid-1960s. For some the 1964 and 1965 legislation brought fulfillment of great dreams, particularly in southern counties where blacks became a voting majority. In most areas of the country, though, there was no possibility of blacks constituting the enfranchised majority. Progress would have to be made as a minority group. And the single greatest barrier to that progress after 1965 was the cultural hostility of much of white America. While the legislation of 1964 and 1965 granted certain rights, it did not create a culturally more pluralistic society. American media, primary and secondary school curricula, indeed the whole national culture continued to exhibit a strong cultural bias against blacks. In the 1930s, W. E. B. Du Bois had lamented that, "in propaganda against the Negro since emancipation in this land, we face one of the most stupendous efforts the world ever saw to discredit human beings involving universities, history, science, social life and religion."[27] The legislation of 1964 and 1965 could do nothing to redress that persistent culture of racism. It was this problem Martin

Luther King, Jr. had in mind when he commented, "Morality cannot be legislated."[28]

Black Power addressed problems of American culture that were beyond the reach of legal structures. It sought, first and foremost, to change the way whites and blacks saw each other as people, not just as citizens. When Willie Ricks and Stokely Carmichael shouted "Black Power" in Mississippi in 1966, a younger generation of black intellectuals and radicals served notice that they were going to challenge the cultural supports of American racism.[29] Black Power advocates sought this cultural reform because they recognized the perverse effects that white collective memory had on blacks. In an interview with Robert Penn Warren, Stokely Carmichael (chairman of SNCC from 1966–69) voiced the familiar lament that white cultural hegemony had taken a great toll on black identity.

> *Warren:* How commonly do you think the Negro may accept some derogatory stereotype of himself? . . .
>
> *Carmichael:* It's very common, because whether Negroes admit it or not, they are one hundred and fifty percent American. They think, they act, they accept America without even questioning it.
>
> *Warren:* Including the white man's version of himself—the Negro?
>
> *Carmichael:* Including that, I'm afraid.[30]

And in 1967, in his book *Black Power,* co-authored with Charles V. Hamilton, Carmichael confirmed that cultural change was the heart of the Black Power agenda. Chapter 2 of *Black Power,* entitled "Its Need and Substance," states the goal: "Our basic need is to reclaim our history and our identity from what must be called cultural terrorism."[31]

Carmichael, like generations of black intellectuals before him, regarded memory as a central support for white cultural hegemony. By attacking white collective memory, Carmichael believed, blacks could destroy the larger culture of racism which continued to hold them back. The bold radicalism of Black Power demonstrated to black people that they could assert themselves in the arena of national culture. In countless locations across America, people inspired by the rhetoric of Black Power publicly asserted their heritage.

The enormous preoccupation with the issue of collective memory in the late 1960s and early 1970s is not a phenomenon that can be observed only in retrospect. Contemporary observers saw it as well. Writing in 1971, sociologist Orlando Patterson observed:

> One of the striking features of the current Black activism is the strong emphasis placed upon history both as an end in itself and as a means towards the attainment of critical psychological, cultural, and political goals . . . [T]he present Black movement in the U.S. is perhaps singular in the intensity of its involvement with the past and in demands made upon history for the affirmation of racial pride and dignity. This concern exists at all levels, from the semi-literate ghetto housewife attending a community-based cultural workshop to the large number of intellectuals and graduate students writing dissertations or popular works on the subject.[32]

In the late 1960s black Americans began to assert their heritage forcefully, but they also began to debate among themselves, with greater vigor than ever before, exactly what black heritage was in the first place. This debate continues to the present day and has given rise to a variety of viewpoints, two of which will be examined in some detail. First is the Afrocentric position, which holds that while black achievement in America is considerable, African history is still supremely important for developing black self-esteem. This vision of history contrasts with what will be referred to here as the "Americanist" interpretation of black history. Americanists believe that the

black experience in this country is of sufficient depth and grandeur to
make reference to Africa unnecessary for black self-esteem.

Afrocentrism and Collective Memory

In every generation of this century there have been black intellectuals
who have argued that black self-esteem would be best served by emphasizing American blacks' connection to Africa. While there has always been near-universal consensus among black intellectuals about
the desirability of affirming the achievements of blacks in America,
the usefulness of African heritage has provoked heated debate. The
issue, as it has been articulated by black thinkers for generations, is
whether or not American blacks can make something useful out of
the history and culture of a place that the vast majority of them will
never see.

The modern founding father of Afrocentrism, Marcus Garvey, argued passionately for a reinvigoration of the black American connection to Africa.[33] In his essay, "Who and What Is a Negro?" (1923),
Garvey wrote:

> The white world has always tried to rob and discredit us of our
> history . . . Every student of history, of impartial mind, knows
> that the Negro once ruled the world, when white men were
> savages and barbarians living in caves; that thousands of Negro
> professors at that time taught in the universities in Alexandria,
> then the seat of learning, that Egypt gave the world civilization
> and that Greece and Rome have robbed Egypt of her art and
> letters, and taken all the credit to themselves.[34]

Garvey argued for an aggressive program to reclaim the past, exhort-
ing blacks to write their "own interpretation of scripture and history."[35] He admonished them: "Never allow false statements or allegations against your race to become current and pass into history, as
if it [sic] were a fact."[36]

Garvey's Afrocentric program may sound like a call for empirical rigor, but nothing could be farther from the truth. In *Lessons from the School of Philosophy,* he explained that because "[t]he white man is a great propagandist," blacks must create their "own propaganda and hand it down the ages."[37] Garvey then offered a programmatic statement for those who wished to use the past, particularly the African past, to improve black self-esteem. "Your entire obsession must be to see things from the Negro's point of view, remembering always that you are a Negro striving for Negro supremacy in every department of life, so that any truth you see or any facts you gather must be twisted to suit the Negro psychology of things . . . Even if you cannot prove it, always claim the Negro was great."[38]

A generation after Garvey, in 1965, Malcolm X gave a speech on Afro-American history in which he attributed many of the problems blacks were then facing to their ignorance of history, and African history in particular:

> And the thing that has kept most of us, that is, the Afro-Americans, almost crippled in this society has been our complete lack of knowledge concerning the past. The number one thing that makes us different from other people is our lack of knowledge concerning the past. Proof of which—almost anyone can come into this country and get around barriers and obstacles that we cannot get around; and the only difference between them and us, they know something about the past, and in knowing something about the past, they know something about themselves, they have an identity.[39]

Like many Afrocentrists, Malcolm X lamented that white hegemony had caused a general forgetfulness of Africa among American blacks. In his speeches on history he described the "tricks" that white historiography had played on black memory of Africa: "History has been so 'whitened' by the white man that even the black professors have known little more than the most ignorant black man about the talents and rich civilizations and cultures of the black man in the millenniums ago."[40] Addressing the issue of self-esteem, Malcolm X said: "What made us feel helpless was our hatred for ourselves. And our hatred of ourselves stemmed from our hatred for things African."[41] Thus he believed that black Americans would overcome their identity crisis and learn to love themselves once they gained more knowledge of their heritage, the ancient civilizations of Africa. Malcolm X thought that Africa-centered, historically aware self-love was essential for the liberation of black Americans. Of all the cultural products of the 1960s, none addressed that need more explicitly than the Afrocentric holiday Kwanzaa.

Maulana (Ron) Karenga introduced Kwanzaa in Los Angeles in 1966. Today it is celebrated nationally each December.[42] Karenga established the holiday with the goal of infusing black American life with affirmative historical images from African history. As he explained in a recent book, "Kwanzaa is not a religious holiday, but a cultural one."[43] Karenga's conception of the holiday reflects a deep concern for positive representation of blacks while displaying a marked lack of regard for historical fact. At the holiday's inception he said, "In terms of history, all we need at this point is heroic images, the white boy got enough dates for everybody."[44] Karenga believed that glowing images of black history in Africa could provide a positive basis for black self-worth in America, a usable past. In the *Quotable Karenga,* he explains that for a people to have a sense of themselves (a culture), they must have, first and foremost, "Mythology."[45] Kwanzaa, as Karenga conceived it, was thus designed to propagate and celebrate a set of myths about Africa.

Karenga explains that Kwanzaa "is a project which requires recovering lost models and memory, suppressed principles and practices of African culture."[46] In particular, it satisfies a need for a sense of definite ancestry which he believes the legacy of slavery denies American blacks. Kwanzaa attempts to make up for the absence of any direct black American connection to African ancestors and culture by celebrating a carefully selected collection of African heroes. Karenga says that "Afrocentricity at its cultural best is an ongoing quest for [a] historical and cultural anchor."[47] Karenga's anchor, like Garvey's, is the African (and Egyptian) past. Kwanzaa provides a heroic African past to black Americans who feel the need for a history that goes beyond America. The holiday is thus an invented tradition which satisfies the desire (not at all unique to American blacks) for a deeply affirmative sense of heritage in a rootless world. Karenga's hope for Kwanzaa is that its Afrocentric myths will, when collectively believed and acted upon by all people of African ancestry, "restore our people to their traditional greatness."[48]

Another leading proponent of Afrocentrism today, Molefi Kete Asante (born Arthur L. Smith, Jr.), chairman of Temple University's Department of African-American Studies, also explicitly claims that myths have great potential to solve the problems of black Americans. In *Kemet, Afrocentricity and Knowledge,* he says that empowering myths "will be the resolution of ethnic conflict."[49] And in *Afrocentricity* he writes that "[c]onsciousness precedes unity."[50] For Asante, unity is key to the material improvement of black life in America. And, like Karenga, Asante thinks that Afrocentric history should be composed of any "symbols which validate our interests."[51] Garvey's legacy thus lives on in contemporary attempts to liberate the living by manipulating the past.

Afrocentrists like Karenga and Asante claim that when American blacks achieve a sense of pan-African unity, political liberation will naturally follow. Part of this reasoning is inescapably true. As more and more blacks become attracted to the invented traditions of Kwanzaa and to the very name "African American," the relevance of Africa will of course increase for them. Moreover, as we have seen, traditions can be invented and claims of ethnic identity are self-legitimating. So, eventually, the history of Africa (both real and imagined) may become dominant in black American collective memory. If this occurs, one could reasonably assert that American black identity

will have changed. The political implications of such a change remain
open to debate. Suffice it to say, a great deal of the Afrocentric hope
of liberation hinges on changing the collective consciousness of black
Americans.

Although many see great promise in Afrocentrism, black intellectuals have made two general criticisms of the movement. The first centers on the perceived falsities it proffers. Martin Luther King, Jr., for
example, thought that black Americans had no enduring connection to
Africa. He said, "The Negro is an American. We know nothing of
Africa. He's got to face the fact that he is an American."[52] Many since
King have been more reluctant to reject the African connection entirely, but have been put off by Afrocentrism's explicitly anti-empirical
stance. Henry Louis Gates, Jr., for instance, though he sometimes describes himself as an Afrocentrist, distances himself from the mytholo-
gizing endorsed by Karenga and Asante: "The truth is, too many people
still regard African-American studies primarily as a way to rediscover a
lost cultural identity—or invent one that never quite existed."[53]

However, the charge that much of Afrocentric thought is fanciful
is considered irrelevant by Afrocentrists themselves, who explicitly
reject empiricism as a manifestation of what Maulana Karenga calls
"the progressive Europeanization of human consciousness."[54] More
significant for them is a second critique—that Afrocentrism will not
deliver on its promise of black liberation. A number of black intellectuals have argued that the problems which the black poor continue to
face cannot be solved by further changes in black American consciousness. Historian Clarence Walker, for example, begins his critique of Afrocentrism by placing its promise in historical context.

In the 1920s black people used the trope "new Negro" to describe themselves and signal a break with a painful past. In the
1960s and 1970s we became "black" and "Afro-American,"
abandoning the denomination "Negro," and in the 1990s some
of us have become "African-Americans." These changes in name

tell us that the history of the Negro in North America involves a belief that changes in nomenclature can confer pride and also alter or refashion reality.[55]

Whatever benefits the other changes may have conferred in the past, Walker is skeptical of the liberating power of this latest attempt at group redefinition:

> Afrocentrism can provide no answers to these basic problems [of the black poor] because it theorizes that the social dislocation of the black underclass has its roots in a failure to develop self-esteem. This is nonsense . . . What black people need today is a usable present, not a usable past. But by making black inequality a problem of the mind, Afrocentrism obscures more than it explicates.[56]

Certainly there can be no question that America's current cultural pluralism has facilitated economic advancement for many minorities. As white hegemonic structures became more receptive to peoples of different races, tangible gains were made. Walker claims, though, that there are some very real limits to the power of cultural affirmation to ameliorate structural problems in society. Improvements in self-esteem, made through the rewriting of history, can carry minorities only so far. Walker even suggests that Afrocentrism may actually hurt the truly disadvantaged by drawing attention away from the basic material problems that endure in America.

Other black intellectuals have expressed similar thoughts. In a book on the American collective memory of Malcolm X, media critic Michael Eric Dyson suggests that while Afrocentrism has yielded benefits in the past by empowering many blacks, the most recent expression of popular Afrocentrism—the 1990s Malcolm X fad sparked by Spike Lee's film biography—"is cultural rather than political."[57] Dyson argues that this "cultural renaissance of Malcolm X also embodies the paradoxical nature of black nationalist politics over the past two decades: those most aided by its successes have rarely stuck around to witness the misery of those most hurt by its failures."[58]

The symbols of identity available in mainstream Afrocentrism are meaningful for many blacks of all social classes. The political critique that black intellectuals offer is that Afrocentrism has paid too much attention to symbols and too little to structural issues such as class. Clarence Walker specifically decries what he regards as an Afrocentric obsession with symbols: "The problems of the black underclass have more to do with issues of structural inequality than a failure on the part of black Americans to be proud or to know their history."[59] Looking back on the Malcolm X fad of the early 1990s, one Harvard student offered what may be the most concise criticism of popular Afrocentrism: "I wore the hat, but nothing happened."[60]

In an article published in 1971, Orlando Patterson voiced an early skepticism about the liberating power of Afrocentric history. "[I]t is sometimes possible to ask too much of history. If, under our present circumstances, we cannot achieve a status which, by itself, ensures our pride, then no amount of wistful looking back will help us. All we should do then is to make our past the sand in which we hide our heads."[61] More than twenty-five years later, it should be clear that Afrocentrism has conveyed cultural benefits and meaning to many, while remaining a controversial historical vision. Black intellectuals have criticized Afrocentrism both for its anti-empiricism and for obscuring the real needs of the black poor. Thus history can serve as a resource to achieve contemporary goals, but, as the various critics of Afrocentrism suggest, those who focus too long on the past may undermine their ability to act in the present.

Americanist Black History

The representation of black history in schools, museums, and other knowledge-producing institutions has expanded dramatically since the 1960s. The focus of this expansion has been the celebration of

Americanist black history rather than Afrocentric history. While not necessarily indifferent to African history, Americanists adhere to Martin Luther King's position that a positive sense of black identity is best grounded in the achievements of blacks in this country. If Afrocentrism remains a controversial and relatively marginalized vision of black history, the Americanist interpretation is now quite mainstream.[62]

The representation of Americanist black history has developed only in the last thirty years. In fact, less than a dozen black-history museums were created in the ninety years following the Civil War. Although scores of historical sites existed, few were specifically run as museums, and none of them had the resources to present a comprehensive overview of black history.[63] The DuSable Museum of African American History (originally the Ebony Museum) opened in Chicago in 1961 and claims to be the oldest African American museum in America.[64] In the sense that the museum is devoted to black history in general, rather than to a particular event or person, its claim appears to be accurate.

The representation of black history has expanded dramatically since the mid-1960s. In the thirty-year period since the Voting Rights Act, well over one hundred museums devoted specifically to black history have been created. A directory of black museums indicates that more than fifty were founded in the 1970s. Thirty more museums were founded in the 1980s, a decade generally remembered for its cultural conservatism.[65] Many of these museums are modest affairs which attempt to present only the events associated with a particular historic structure, like the African American Meeting House in Boston (1974) or the Herndon Home in Atlanta (1977). Others, such as the Wilberforce Afro-American Museum and Cultural Center in Ohio (1971) and Museum of African American History in Detroit (1987), are multi-million dollar institutions with the space to present the larger history of black America.

Since the Race Pride Movement was itself made possible by the advances of the Civil Rights Movement, it is not surprising that the most popular subject of black history museums today is Civil Rights. The events of that period are commemorated at small sites which have been open to the public since the early days of the movement, like the Dexter Avenue-King Memorial Baptist Church in Montgomery and the Sixteenth St. Baptist Church in Birmingham. The larger history of the movement is the subject of several multi-million dollar museums that have opened in the 1990s, such as the Birmingham Civil Rights Museum (1991), the Memphis Civil Rights Museum (1992), and the Martin Luther King, Jr. Museum in Atlanta (1996).

Americanist black history has become a common feature of the country's historical landscape and collective memory. But while this expansion has been impressive, it has not occurred without political struggle. If the Americanist vision of black history is now well represented in America, it is only because black Americans fought to make it so. Thus the analysis now turns to the practical politics of expanding American collective memory. In particular, the focus will be on the politics of commemorating and interpreting the life of Martin Luther King, Jr., honored today with both a national holiday and a shrine at his birth home in Atlanta.

The Martin Luther King, Jr. National Holiday

Black Americans were the initial catalyst for the Race Pride Movement and their impact on American collective memory has been greater than that of any other group. The centrality of blacks in the transformation of American memory is well illustrated by the national holiday for Martin Luther King, Jr., the only American for whom we have a national holiday.[66] By contrast, George Washington, Thomas Jefferson, and Abraham Lincoln are now honored only on the generic Presidents' Day. King's elevation to this unique status was the result of more than a decade of direct political action by black Americans.

The idea for the holiday first emerged during the period of national mourning for King's death. Four days after the assassination, Representative John Conyers of Michigan introduced legislation for a national holiday. Without any serious organization to push it through, the bill failed to make it out of committee. After that initial defeat, however, organized support for the holiday developed quickly. Later in 1968, the Southern Christian Leadership Conference (SCLC) endorsed Conyers's idea. Ralph Abernathy, King's replacement as head of the SCLC, met with President-elect Richard Nixon to discuss the holiday idea. Abernathy reported that Nixon offered encouragement and the SCLC continued to lobby for the holiday over the next few years, even gathering a petition with three million signatures by the summer of 1971.[67]

Regardless of what Nixon might have said to Abernathy, the Nixon administration was actually firmly opposed to the holiday proposal. One reason for this opposition was that Nixon understood that his election was made possible in part by anti-black sentiment in America.[68] In an effort to clinch the Southern conservative vote, Nixon had selected as his running mate former Maryland Governor Spiro Agnew, an opportunistic segregationist.[69] When Nixon was elected in 1968, the Race Pride Movement had yet to achieve the enormous legitimacy it has today. Nixon could therefore oppose any plans for the holiday without fear of risking essential votes.

Another reason for the Nixon administration's opposition to the holiday was F.B.I. Director J. Edgar Hoover. Nixon's election in 1968 was sweet vindication for Hoover, a long-time enemy of King. Hoover's hatred of King went back many years and extended well beyond a distaste for the man's politics. During the 1960s Hoover had King under constant surveillance and attempted to intimidate the Civil Rights leadership with allegations of sexual impropriety and communist influence.[70] While these intrigues are common knowledge today, less familiar is Hoover's pursuit of his obsession beyond King's death.

Nixon's meeting with Abernathy about the holiday idea alarmed Hoover, who took it upon himself to brief the President and his staff on the "real" King. Hoover rightly judged that the Republican leadership, especially Spiro Agnew, would be receptive to the idea of maligning King's character. On January 23, 1969, just ten days after Nixon and Abernathy met, Hoover sent a memo to the new Attorney General, John Mitchell, explaining his intention to discredit King: "The Southern Christian Leadership Conference, founded by Martin Luther King, Jr., held demonstrations on January 15, 1969, King's birthday, urging that his birthday be made a national holiday . . . In view of this, there is enclosed a document regarding the communist influence on King during his career . . . For your information, a copy of this document is also being furnished to the President."[71] Hoover personally delivered to Nixon additional material on King's "highly immoral behavior."[72] John Ehrlichman later recalled Hoover's explicit theorizing about King's actions. According to Hoover, King's "basic problem was that he liked white girls."[73] William Sullivan claimed that Hoover referred to King as a "burr head."[74] Hoover's hatred for King continued until Hoover's death in 1972, and it was this hatred that motivated his lobbying against the King holiday. As John Ehrlichman explained, "It was pretty obvious. He [Hoover] was trying to rewrite history . . . In the great marketplace of ideas, Hoover was trying to establish a position on the civil rights issue by impugning the morality and rectitude of Martin Luther King."[75]

The King holiday idea had powerful enemies in 1970, but King's hold on the national consciousness was to prove greater than Hoover's ability to besmirch his reputation. Although Hoover's accusations found receptive ears in the Nixon White House, even the F.B.I. later came to regret Hoover's actions. During the Ford administration two separate Justice Department task forces reevaluated the Hoover assault on King. The first review was conducted by Assistant

Attorney General J. Stanley Pottinger. After examining Hoover's
files in 1976, he issued a statement describing Hoover's investigation
of King as "scurrilous and immaterial to any proper law enforcement
function or historic purpose."[76] The second assessment, made by Justice Department attorney Fred Folsom, came to the same conclusion.
All of the Hoover files on King were subsequently sealed until
2027.[77]

Outside the executive branch, the King holiday idea continued to
build support during the Nixon years. Illinois (1973) and Massachusetts (1974) both made King's birthday a state holiday.[78] After
Hoover's death in 1972, and once the Watergate furor had passed,
the holiday idea slowly began to gain favor. Beginning in 1978, a series of King birthday marches on Washington were organized in support of the holiday. The largest of these, in 1980, brought over
100,000 people to Washington to hear King's widow, Coretta Scott
King, speak and entertainers like Stevie Wonder perform in support
of the holiday. The celebration in Washington was paralleled by efforts around the country. In early 1981 the Martin Luther King, Jr.
Center for Nonviolent Social Change, located in Atlanta, produced
and distributed a national petition, eventually gathering over seven
million signatures.[79] Later that year California became the third
state to establish a King holiday.[80] Momentum for the holiday was
building.

In Congress the holiday legislation was reintroduced every year
from 1968 by Representative Conyers.[81] In 1979 the King Holiday
Bill passed in the House, only to fail to reach the floor of the Senate.
The House vote provided a rallying point for supporters of the holiday. In 1983, on the twentieth anniversary of the March on Washington, the majority of the GOP hierarchy endorsed the legislation and
President Ronald Reagan promised to sign it. It passed in the House
by a vote of 338 to 90 and in the Senate by 78 to 22. Ronald Reagan
signed the holiday legislation into law on November 2, 1983, as
Coretta Scott King and a host of civil rights leaders looked on. The

first observance of the federal holiday was on January 20, 1986. Since 1983 all remaining state legislatures except New Hampshire have enacted similar state holiday laws.[82]

The bipartisan support for the King holiday suggests that by the mid-1980s the celebration of Americanist black heritage was no longer controversial. Even former foes of King, such as South Carolina Senator Strom Thurmond, supported the holiday. At the time of the passage of the holiday bill, Thurmond explained that he wanted to show his "respect for the important contributions of our minority citizens."[83] An expression of such sentiments from a man who once ran as the presidential candidate for the white-supremacist Dixiecrat Party illustrates just how much America has changed in the past few decades. Affirmation of Americanist black heritage has become a normal part of public discourse, which only a small number of people continue to actively oppose.

The celebration of Martin Luther King, Jr. is now a national commonplace, but that does not, per se, tell us very much about how Martin Luther King is actually remembered. One assumption of this work is that memories which become embedded in physical space are somehow more powerful than those which find no material manifestation. Thus, to better understand how America remembers King, the discussion now turns to the interpretation of his life's work presented at the Martin Luther King, Jr. National Historic Site in Atlanta.

The Martin Luther King, Jr. National Historic Site

In the late 1970s, when considerable support had already developed for creating a national holiday for King, King's family, working with the National Park Service, suggested making his birth home and the surrounding neighborhood a national historic site. Because political consensus was about to make the holiday a reality, the much less expensive proposal for a historic site breezed through Congress with bipartisan support in 1979. The federal site created in Atlanta includes King's birth home, tomb, parts of the Sweet Auburn neighborhood where he grew up, and a museum interpreting his life. The King shrine is the premier black history pilgrimage site in America, and the most important physical representation of the Race Pride vision in the American historical landscape. The shrine receives more visitors annually than the birth homes of Kennedy, Washington, and Lincoln combined.[84] Presidents and foreign dignitaries regularly appear at the site for speeches and tours. The existence and enormous popularity of the King site are additional evidence of the mainstreaming of the Americanist interpretation of black history.

The federal interpretation of King at the site has been shaped most by the expectation that King will in fact be celebrated. This expectation has encouraged Park Service interpreters to emphasize themes in King's life which are most popular with Americans. Chief Historian Dean Rowley, who has been at the site since its opening in the early 1980s, describes the Park Service's approach to the King story: "When we first moved out here on site, we had a historian working here who was used to being in intellectual circles where you tell the absolute truth, and he got into trouble with something he said. And the lady who was superintendent at the time said, 'The Park Service does non-controversial history.'"[85] The phrase "non-controversial history" appears often in conversation with National Park Service historians across the country. Rangers often refer to the necessity of offering historical interpretations that are in "good taste."[86] "Good taste," in turn, can be shown to have consistently affected what is and is not said about King at the historic site.

During the early years of the Park Service's management of the site, the Civil Rights Movement was still considered controversial. The presentation of King's life accordingly avoided the tough issues of segregation and American racism. Rather, attention was placed solely on King's childhood in Sweet Auburn. The Chief of Interpretation for the site, Gayle Hazelwood, explained, "Right now what

we do is what I refer to as the happy boyhood tours. We parade
people through the home . . . It's very sanitized."[87] Eventually, this
avoidance of the Civil Rights era was judged politically unnecessary
and the staff began the work which culminated in the 1996 King
museum.

The museum that the Park Service opened in 1996 includes thorough coverage of King's civil rights activism. The museum traces his
career from the Birmingham Bus Boycott to the "I Have a Dream"
speech to his assassination in 1968. The fact that the federal government now regards segregation and discrimination as valid subjects for
discussion at public institutions suggests that they are no longer controversial or risky. Rather, these topics are now fashionable, in "good
taste." Further evidence for this comes from the Civil Rights museums in Birmingham and Memphis.

The Birmingham and Memphis museums are significant models for
the King museum, and it is worthwhile to consider the examples they
set. Outside the Birmingham museum bronze police dogs bark at the
innocent and a bronze water hose points at huddled children. Inside,
the museum has functioning segregated water fountains (less water
spurts from the "colored" one). Both the Memphis and Birmingham
museums prominently display a bombed freedom bus. (The buses are
replicas which have been burned for exhibition.) Such patterns indi-
cate that as the drama of the Civil Rights era passes from living memory into the collective past, the memories are becoming acceptable,
even commonplace.

The Birmingham and Memphis museums present the past as a simple black-white conflict. Neither museum seriously addresses the
ways in which black and white identities were dialectically formed.
Instead, they reinforce the prevalent belief that black and white
Americans have little in common historically except mutual antipa-
thy. Although they both offer the hope and promise of racial harmony
in the present and future, these museums indirectly support the view
that race is the only variable which matters in American history.

Since the Civil Rights Movement and American racism are now mainstream subjects, more of Martin Luther King's life story is now covered at the Atlanta site. However, "good taste" still necessitates downplaying the parts of his legacy that do not meet public expectations. Thus, there is thorough coverage of King's life to the triumphs of 1964 and 1965, but more selective presentation of the last three years of his life. This is important because in those last years King developed political commitments which transcended race. Chief Historian for the King site, Dean Rowley, explains: "Nobody has dealt with the last three years of King's life precisely because that is the most socially revolutionary part of his life."[88]

In the years after the Voting Rights Act, King came to believe that the black poor had been left behind by the Civil Rights Movement. He began to preach the need for a national movement to help the poor of all races. Before 1965, King had often prophesied America's doom if it continued to leave unfulfilled its promise to blacks. After 1965, King issued the same warning in the name of all Americans living in poverty. His last political action was organizing a Poor People's March on Washington, which he hoped would do for the poor of all races what the 1963 March had done for civil rights. Bernard Lee, one of King's advisers, later said that it was this class radicalism which "the powers of the country will kill you for."[89] And indeed, shortly before the first organized working-class march on Washington since the Great Depression, Martin Luther King, Jr. was assassinated. With his death, America may have been allowed to dodge some fundamental questions that have since gone unanswered. Certainly King posed a challenge which can still give pause to those who profess to honor his memory and his commitment to social justice. He wrote in "A Time to Break Silence": "True compassion is more than flinging a coin to a beggar; it is not haphazard and superficial. It comes to see that an edifice which produces beggars needs restructuring."[90]

King's championing of the poor transcended all race and ethnic boundaries. In fact, in his last book, *Where Do We Go from Here?: Chaos*

or Community, King even accused the black middle class of betraying
the black poor.

> [A]ll too many members of the Negro middle class have been
> detached spectators rather than involved participants in the
> great drama of social change taking place on the stage of Ameri-
> can history . . . [M]any middle-class Negroes have forgotten
> their roots and are more concerned about "conspicuous con-
> sumption" than about the cause of justice. Instead, they seek to
> sit in some serene and passionless realm of isolation, untouched
> and unmoved by the agonies and struggles of their underprivi-
> leged brothers. This kind of selfish detachment has caused the
> masses of Negroes to feel alienated not only from white society
> but also from the Negro middle class. They feel that the average
> middle-class Negro has no concern for their plight.

> The feeling is often corroborated by the hard facts of experi-
> ence.[91]

Not surprisingly, this language was unpopular with both the white
and black middle class and elite.[92]

King's post-1965 class activism has proved very difficult for the
Civil Rights museums to handle. None makes mention of King's critique of the black middle class. Dean Rowley explains the awkward
position of the nearly all-black staff at the Atlanta site: "I think Dr.
King's always been closer to being an outright revolutionary than
most people want to admit. That is also something that I know good
and well that nobody in the Park Service is going to want to come
right out and say. We know the things that when we talk to them
[visitors] we are going to get into huge fights."[93] Hosea Williams, one
of Martin Luther King's closest associates, has discussed America's
inability to address the totality of King's legacy. Referring in particular to the tendency of Americans to forget those last three years, he
says, "There is a definite effort on the part of America to change

Martin Luther King, Jr. from what he really was all about—to make him the Uncle Tom of the century. To me, he was the radical of the century."[94]

The celebration of race identity and civil rights is no longer radical; rather, it is the norm. But, if the Civil Rights museums in Birmingham and Memphis and the National Park Service site in Atlanta may be taken as representative, the forgetfulness of King's class radicalism is also commonplace.

Conclusions

Collective memory activism began with black Americans and not some other minority group because black leaders and intellectuals had devoted a full century of attention to the question of memory before the 1960s. The explosion of black memory activism in the 1960s was the actualization of a dream long held and historically well articulated. Frederick Douglass, W. E. B. Du Bois, and others had warned about the dangers of forgetting the past, and figures such as Malcolm X and Stokely Carmichael remembered that admonition. Black Power effected a major change in American consciousness. It also sparked the Race Pride Movement, providing the inspiration for similar efforts by other minorities in America.

Black Power gave rise to two different visions of black heritage, the Afrocentric and the Americanist. Afrocentrism has generated a popular holiday, Kwanzaa, and a renewed sense of origin for many black Americans. Yet many black intellectuals have harshly criticized the Afrocentric vision. In addition to its factual errors, they point out that, while there was a time in America when the affirmation of the value of African heritage was politically radical and likely to improve minority lives, more of those celebrations will not help poor families get the things they need to survive. In fact, Afrocentrism may obscure the essential interests of the black poor by suggesting that the amelioration of their suffering will have to wait for the development of a pan-African consciousness. Whatever the merits of this critique, Afrocentrism continues to provide a sense of ancestry for many.

Americanist black history has proved less controversial. Like Afrocentrism, the Americanist vision has produced a secular holiday, for Martin Luther King, Jr. It has also fostered public appreciation of black achievement. Not surprisingly, the Civil Rights Movement has been a popular subject. Major museums in Birmingham, Memphis, and Atlanta now describe the horrors of segregation and the triumphs of the movement. Yet despite its triumphs, Americanist black history has not given us a complete picture of Martin Luther King. Although America has traveled far on the road to a more tolerant society, the forgetfulness of King's later class radicalism suggests how short a distance we have come on the road to the more just society he envisioned.

Conclusion

W
e know ourselves as Americans in large part by what we believe to be true about the nation's past. In the last thirty years there has been a profound change in our understanding of that past, and thus in our identity as a people. Only now are we beginning to appreciate the nature of this change. American collective memory has a diversity today that it did not have thirty years ago, a diversity which is the product of a series of political struggles. People organized in groups across the country to fight for public recognition of minority achievements and of the injustices America has too often inflicted upon its citizens. These efforts have been referred to here as the Race Pride Movement.

The Race Pride Movement addressed problems left unresolved by the earlier Civil Rights Movement. While the Civil Rights Movement dramatically expanded legal representation in America, it did not explicitly address the issue of minority cultural representation. Because the cultural status of groups directly affects the political and economic opportunities of their members, continuing cultural bias left minorities at a distinct disadvantage. Asserting minority cultural identities by transforming the entrenched national perception of their pasts thus became an important goal for many activists.

While this work has focused on the struggle to change the representation of history at national historic sites, other targets of the Race Pride Movement deserve further attention. We need careful studies of the efforts of minorities to expand the presentation of their heritages in schools, universities, the film industry, and other institutions devoted to cultural representation. We also need an analysis of the role whites have played in the movement. As such studies are completed, the magnitude of the Race Pride Movement's achievements will become clearer.

Until now, though, Race Pride has not even been considered a distinct social movement. The large number of minority groups involved in Race Pride and its decentralized structure have prevented recognition of the movement's goal and its accomplishments. Rather, the change in the public perception of minority history has been viewed as part of a vague shift toward cultural pluralism. The problem with this explanation is that representation is guided by power, and changes in the representation of group heritages do not occur without political reason. As these case studies have shown, the transformation of American collective memory that has occurred over the last thirty years was produced by forces which can be described and analyzed.

In the process of changing American memory, Race Pride activists also changed themselves. Indian, Asian American, Latino, and black identities are radically different from what they were thirty years ago. In fact, the self-understandings of all Americans have been powerfully altered. No one race or ethnic group in America can now securely assert that its particular heritage is the one which defines the national identity. There was nothing foreordained about this change. The contemporary expectation, often taken for granted, that our diverse heritages will be represented in schools and museums exists only because minority groups realized the value of their histories and found the strength to assert them before an often hostile nation.

While the accomplishments of the Race Pride Movement are great, not all groups which have participated in the movement have enjoyed equal success. While Indians and blacks produced massive changes in American popular memory, the contributions of Latinos and Asian Americans, though notable, have not been of the same magnitude. The relative success or failure of these groups cannot be attributed so much to organized hostility as to the different ways cultural identities are constructed in America. Asian Americans and

Latinos, for instance, remain deeply divided by the cultural differences among their immigrant populations. Groups which are not united in the present cannot assert unified visions of the past.

Of all American minority groups, it is the two with the longest and most uniform history of being discriminated against—Indians and blacks—which have proved the most effective in asserting new visions of their heritages. The reversal of American attitudes expressed at the Little Bighorn and the creation of a national holiday for Martin Luther King, Jr. both testify to the power that organized groups have to change public perception of their histories. Americans can no longer remember the westward expansion without thinking of the injustices done to Indians, just as we cannot look back on this century without recalling our debt to Martin Luther King, Jr. These memories will endure because Indians and blacks fought to present them to the nation. Their successful struggle for institutional representation improved their cultural status in the present by expanding public recognition of the value of their pasts.

The Civil Rights Movement expanded political representation by changing laws. Building on that achievement, the Race Pride Movement expanded cultural representation by altering the institutions which control the presentation of the past. Because of these movements, American society is more inclusive than at any point in its history. This very success, however, raises some important questions about the future.

Because memories of terrible injustices are now central to the self-understanding of many minorities, it is necessary to ask whether the identities built around those memories are fated to remain oppositional. It is not obvious that recognition of the value of minority heritages by the majority will thereby enable those minorities to have a sense of inclusion. Given their memories of past oppression, many may feel marginal even among populations which respect and value their heritage. It remains an open question whether minority groups can simultaneously assert their memories of oppression and also feel at home with the majority. If minority identities are to be other than oppositional, minorities themselves will have to grapple with the anxieties and fears that their past oppression can easily inspire.

This leads to a larger question about the future of the nation. Is it possible for America to achieve a coherent and positive national identity? If it is true that we understand the present through our memories of the past, then we are always in danger of allowing the political questions of our time to be framed in terms borrowed from that past. The contemporary culture wars in America, for instance, may be seen as a struggle over the enduring meaning of history. The battle lines are familiar. Many believe that the racial injustices of the past have left a warped and narrow society. Others think those injustices are historical facts, but that America is now a generally open and tolerant nation. The Race Pride Movement has provided the common ground for this debate by expanding public recognition of minority heritages, including the injustices minorities have endured. Ironically, though, the new public history may have the negative effect of obscuring the real achievements of the last thirty years. Our memories may now be undermining our ability to progress as a people.

Many in our country believe that it is the lack of national recognition of minority cultures which explains the persistence of gross inequalities in our society. Perhaps they fail to recognize the degree to which the Race Pride Movement has already triumphed in public discourse. Its images are now established in our minds and fixed in our historical landscape. Those who hope for a more just society will have to look beyond Race Pride.

NOTES

INTRODUCTION

1. "For John F. Kennedy His Inauguration," in *The Poetry of Robert Frost* (New York: Holt, Rinehart and Winston, 1969), p. 422. Frost read this new poem as a preface to his older poem, "The Gift Outright."

2. Maya Angelou, "On the Pulse of Morning" (New York: Random House, 1993), np.

3. Frost, p. 424.

4. Angelou, np. I have not retained the enjambments or capitalizations of the original.

5. The term "collective memory" is most closely associated with the French sociologist Maurice Halbwachs. For an introduction to his work see Maurice Halbwachs, *On Collective Memory,* ed. and trans. Lewis A. Coser (Chicago: The University of Chicago Press, 1992).

6. Charles Taylor also makes this point in "The Politics of Representation." He explains that "a person or group can suffer real damage, real distortion, if the people or society around them mirror back to them a conflicting or demeaning or contemptible picture of themselves. Nonrecognition or misrecognition can inflict harm, can be a form of oppression." In Charles Taylor et al., *Multiculturalism,* ed. Amy Gutmann (Princeton: Princeton University Press, 1994), p. 25.

7. See, for example, Doug McAdam, *Political Process and the Development of Black Insurgency, 1930–1970* (Chicago: University of Chicago Press, 1982), pp. 181–229.

8. The literature on these small groups is quite extensive, suggesting that their significance transcends their individual achievements. See Vine Deloria, Jr., *Behind the Trail of Broken Treaties: An Indian Declaration of Independence* (Austin: University of Texas Press, 1985); William Wei, *The Asian American Movement* (Philadelphia: Temple University Press, 1993);

Carlos Muñoz, Jr., *Youth, Identity, Power: The Chicano Movement* (London: Verso, 1989); and Clayborne Carson, *In Struggle: SNCC and the Black Awakening of the 1960s* (Cambridge: Harvard University Press, 1981).

9. For a detailed analysis of the resource mobilization pattern in the Civil Rights Movement, see McAdam, *Political Process*.

10. Robert Penn Warren, *The Legacy of the Civil War: Meditations on the Centennial* (New York: Random House, 1961), p. 78.

1. AMERICAN INDIANS

1. Robert Frost, "The Gift Outright," in *The Poetry of Robert Frost* (New York: Holt, Rinehart, and Winston, 1969), p. 425.

2. Maya Angelou, "On the Pulse of Morning" (New York: Random House, 1993), np.

3. Roderick Nash, *Wilderness and the American Mind,* 3d ed. (New Haven: Yale University Press, 1982), p. 251. Nash identifies the youth of the 1960s as the first generation to identify more strongly with nature than with the march-of-progress narrative.

4. Richard Slotkin, *The Fatal Environment: The Myth of the Frontier in the Age of Industrialization* (New York: Atheneum, 1985), p. 531.

5. For a concise history of events since 1890, see James S. Olson and Raymond Wilson, *Native Americans in the Twentieth Century* (Urbana: University of Illinois Press, 1984).

6. Stephen Cornell, *The Return of the Native: American Indian Political Resurgence* (New York: Oxford University Press, 1988), pp. 167–169.

7. Vine Deloria, Jr., *Behind the Trail of Broken Treaties: An Indian Declaration of Independence* (Austin: University of Texas Press, 1985), p. 25.

8. Ibid., p. 41. The slogan Red Power, derived from Black Power, first appeared in connection with the National Indian Youth Council in 1969. Alvin M. Josephy, Jr., *Now That the Buffalo's Gone: A Study of Today's American Indians* (New York: Alfred A. Knopf, 1982), p. 228.

9. Deloria, p. 34.

10. The historiography of Jewish resistance at Masada offers an interesting parallel to the Indian case. See Barry Schwartz, "The Recovery of

Masada: A Study in Collective Memory," *Sociological Quarterly* 27 (Summer 1986), pp. 147–164.

11. Deloria, p. 41.
12. Ibid.
13. Because of this rapprochement, the emotional distance between urban and reservation Indians is not nearly so great as it once was. Cornell, p. 144.
14. Peter Matthiessen, *In the Spirit of Crazy Horse* (New York: Viking Press, 1983), p. 39.
15. The Alcatraz takeover was a small affair. When federal officials finally seized the island, there were only ten adults and five children present. Josephy, pp. 228–230; Matthiessen, pp. 36–38.
16. Matthiessen, p. 53.
17. Josephy, p. 205.
18. Matthiessen, p. 56.
19. Deloria, p. 61.
20. Means acknowledges that his early politicization was driven by a desire for a sense of heritage and identity. Matthiessen, p. 38.
21. Ibid., pp. 55–56.
22. The buildup to this struggle is described in "The Fight Against Wilson," in *Voices from Wounded Knee, 1973* (Mohawk Nation via Rooseveltown, New York: Akwesasne Note, 1974), pp. 14–21.
23. Robert M. Utley, *The Lance and the Shield: The Life and Times of Sitting Bull* (New York: Henry Holt, 1993), pp. 281–289, 308–311.
24. Matthiessen, p. 66. Chapter 3 of *In the Spirit of Crazy Horse* gives an account of the takeover. Many of the Pine Ridge residents who opposed the takeover were on the payroll of the Tribal Council. The Council received federal money and was thus able to exert considerable influence over the economically depressed reservation. Large numbers of Indians were thus implicated in the generally white-led effort to suppress Indians. Matthiessen explains (pp. 61–62) that this sort of racial co-optation was an enduring feature of life at Pine Ridge, dating back at least to the murder of Sitting Bull by Indian BIA agents in 1890.
25. Olson and Wilson, p. 173.
26. Deloria, p. 78.

27. The army was also involved. General Alexander Haig, acting with Nixon's approval, sent army equipment and advisers to the FBI. Matthiessen, pp. 586–588.

28. Others were killed or wounded in vigilante actions that occurred in the area before and after the takeover. Matthiessen, pp. 60–61; *Voices from Wounded Knee, 1973,* pp. 260–261.

29. Scores of the participants were from cities and other reservations. It is hard, though, to be very precise about the number of people involved. One Indian participant in the shoot-out explained to me that the number fluctuated regularly. Despite the heavy FBI presence, it was apparently not very hard to slip in and out of camp. More than five hundred participants were finally indicted by the FBI. Matthiessen, pp. 81–83.

30. Deloria, p. 80. Continuing the militant defense of land rights, notrespassing signs which say "Why Die?" are still displayed along the borders of the Pine Ridge Reservation.

31. Deloria, pp. 80–81.

32. The Wounded Knee Survivors Association has raised the issue of compensation for descendants at congressional hearings on Indian affairs in 1976, 1990 and 1991. A hearing was also held in 1939 to determine the nature of the events there. *Dakota Times,* 15 May 1991, p. A1; in LBNM files. (Note: In a few instances I take information from the scrapbooks and clippings files stored in the archive of the Little Bighorn National Monument. In some cases the full citation for a newspaper item is not available. If any of the usual information is thus missing, the citation is to the LBNM files.)

33. U.S. Congress, Senate, Select Committee on Indian Affairs, *Wounded Knee Memorial and Historic Site/Little Big Horn National Monument Battlefield, Hearing Before the Select Committee on Indian Affairs,* 101st Cong., 2d sess., 25 September 1990, p. 42.

34. Brian W. Dippie, *Custer's Last Stand: The Anatomy of an American Myth* (Missoula: University of Montana Publications in History, 1976), p. 135.

35. Other than the Little Bighorn, Custer's only other major battle with Indians was at Washita in 1868. For more information, see note 41.

36. For a much longer exposition of the same point, see chap. 18 of Slotkin's *The Fatal Environment*.

37. For a discussion of these films see Dippie, pp. 96–117. Ronald Reagan played the role of Custer in *Santa Fe Trail*. Reagan reminisced fondly about the role and the man in Ronald W. Reagan, "Looking Back at *Santa Fe Trail*," *Greasy Grass* 6 (May 1990), pp. 2–5.

38. Vine Deloria, Jr., *Custer Died for Your Sins: An Indian Manifesto* (New York: Macmillan, 1969), p. 148.

39. For a detailed survey of the way the new history has reconstructed race roles in the old West, see Gerald D. Nash, *Creating the West: Historical Interpretations 1890–1990* (Albuquerque: University of New Mexico Press, 1991), pp. 235–257. Nash argues that many authors have simply replaced one stereotype with another.

40. Dippie, p. 135.

41. Custer's real historical significance is exaggerated in both visions. His only other major battle with Indians was at Washita (present-day Oklahoma) in 1868. Some scholars have argued that Custer ordered an Indian massacre at Washita. See, for example, Stan Hoig's *The Battle of Washita: The Sheridan-Custer Indian Campaign of 1867–69* (New York: Doubleday, 1976). Others have been more generous to Custer. See, for example, Robert M. Utley's *Cavalier in Buckskin: George Armstrong Custer and the Western Military Frontier* (Norman: University of Oklahoma Press, 1988), pp. 64–71. Either way, the single engagement at Washita is thin material with which to build a case for or against Custer.

42. The account in this paragraph draws on material in Douglas C. McChristian, "In Search of Custer Battlefield," *Montana: The Magazine of Western History* 42 (Winter 1992), pp. 75–76.

43. There was one wooden marker for an Indian who fought for the army.

44. The entire interpretive text (that is, the writing on the walls) from the old museum is reproduced in Harry B. Robinson, *Guide to the Custer Battlefield Museum* (Helena, Montana: Naegele Printing Company, 1952).

45. Don Rickey, Jr., *History of Custer Battlefield* (Billings, Montana: Custer Battlefield Historical & Museum Association, 1967), p. 119.

46. Legislation for the construction of a museum was passed in 1939, largely to house the collection of Custer material which Libby Custer

bequeathed to the nation in 1933, with the condition that the government establish a George Custer museum. Funds for the museum were not allocated until after World War II. Rickey, p. 91. For a history of Libby Custer's efforts to memorialize her husband, see Shirley A. Leckie, *Elizabeth Bacon Custer and the Making of a Myth* (Norman: University of Oklahoma Press, 1993).

47. "Custer Battlefield National Cemetery" (Washington, D.C.: National Park Service, ca. 1945), p. 1. Battlefield information brochure. There are multiple editions of battlefield information brochures and guidebooks with textual variations. Brochures are sometimes not dated, but Park Service printing styles change regularly through the years, so no approximation will be off by more than a few years. In no instance does my analysis hinge on a very precise date. Also note that the area was renamed a monument in 1946. The terms cemetery and monument refer to the same 765-acre site. The actual cemetery within the monument today retains the designation Custer National Cemetery.

48. Robert L. Hart, "Changing Exhibitry and Sensitivity: The Custer Battlefield Museum," in *Custer Battlefield Historical & Museum Association Annual Symposium* 1 (1987), p. 37.

49. Hart, p. 36; Robinson, p. 21.

50. "Custer Battlefield National Monument" (Washington, D.C.: National Park Service, ca. 1966), np. Battlefield information brochure.

51. Robert M. Utley, former chief historian at Custer Battlefield, uses the phrase "patriotic orthodoxy" to describe the Park Service's interpretation before 1970. In Robert M. Utley, "Whose Shrine Is It?: The Ideological Struggle for Custer Battlefield," *Montana: The Magazine of Western History* 42 (Winter 1992), p. 72.

52. Text copied from a photograph of the plaque in the LBNM files.

53. "Two-sided Story: Battlefield Will Give Indian Version," *Billings Gazette,* 14 October 1972; in LBNM files.

54. In Edward Tabor Linenthal, *Sacred Ground: Americans and Their Battlefields* (Urbana: University of Illinois Press, 1991), p. 154. This paragraph and the following one are based on Linenthal's summary of documents from the files at the Little Bighorn National Monument.

55. Ibid.

56. Robert M.. Utley, *Custer Battlefield* (Washington, D.C.: Office of Publications, National Park Service, 1968), p. 10. In the 1988 edition of this work, Utley estimates at most 2,000 Indians (p. 65).

57. In Linenthal, p. 142.

58. Ibid. Emphasis added in Linenthal.

59. Ibid.

60. This orientation reached its apogee when the Park Service hired archaeologists to go over every inch of the battlefield with metal detectors, plotting the location of every bullet left on the field. The results of this massive endeavor are related in Richard A. Fox, *Archaeology, History, and Custer's Last Stand: The Little Bighorn Reexamined* (Norman: University of Oklahoma, 1993).

61. In personal interviews, many Park Service interpreters at other sites have described this strategy. Another example is the Vietnam War Memorial, where the Park Service interpretation centers on the construction materials of the memorial itself rather than the war and its meaning.

62. "Indians Stalk Custer Ghost: After 100 Years Wounds of Bighorn Still Festering," *Los Angeles Times,* 25 June 1976; in LBNM files.

63. Ibid.

64. Ibid.

65. Indians had participated in many memorial services before, but always in forms dictated by whites. See chap. 4 of Linenthal's *Sacred Ground* for a summary of previous observances.

66. Richard Hart, "The Superintendent's Speech, 24 June, 1976," in *Custer Centennial Observance 1976,* ed. Michael Koury (Fort Collins, Colorado: The Old Army Press, 1978), p. 35.

67. Robert M. Utley, "Keynote Speech, 24 June, 1976," in *Custer Centennial Observance,* p. 40.

68. Ibid., p. 42. The term "historicism" refers to the view that all ethics are historically contingent, and thus it is inappropriate for one era to judge the morality of another. As the historian David Hackett Fisher explains, historicism "reduces ethics (and much else) to a province of historiography." This, in turn, leads to the "nasty idea that whatever is becoming, is right." Utley's understanding of history was perilously

close to this. David Hackett Fisher, *Historians' Fallacies: Toward a Logic of Historical Thought* (New York: Harper Torchbooks, 1970) p. 156.

69. In *The Blade,* 16 January 1976; in LBNM files.

70. All Park Service sites engage private businesses to run their bookstores so that funds thereby generated do not have to be returned to Washington. The CBHMA was unique in that it was composed of individuals devoted to the history of the site. Most other cooperating organizations are ideologically neutral businesses which share profits with the individual sites.

71. Michael J. Koury, "A Bit of CBHMA History," unpublished speech delivered at the CBHMA annual meeting in Hardin, MT, in 1994. Copy courtesy of the author.

72. Ibid., p. 13.

73. Although the Crow reservation surrounds the battlefield, most of the Custer Battlefield activists have been outsiders. This may be because the Crow fought for the U.S. Army in 1876.

74. Philip Selznick, *TVA and the Grass Roots: A Study in the Sociology of Formal Organizations* (New York: Harper & Row, 1966), p. 73.

75. Kitty Deernose (site archivist at LBNM) interview, July 1994. It should be pointed out that, in the wide spectrum of Custerphiles and nationalists, Court and the chief historian at the time, Neil Mangum, were not promoting the old patriotic orthodoxy. They focused on military history. (After he resigned, Court stayed in the area, offering specialty tours of the battlefield.) Both Court and Mangum were denounced as revisionists by the Little Bighorn Association (LBA), a group devoted to the worship of Custer. For more details see the LBA newsletter collection in the LBNM files.

76. In Linenthal, p. 158.

77. Throughout this chapter I have focused on organized protests. Indians also continued to voice their grievances to park superintendents during the intervening years. For more details, see chap. 4 of Linenthal's *Sacred Ground.*

78. In Wayne Michael Sarf, "Russell Means on Custer Hill," *The American Spectator* 21 (December 1988), p. 32.

79. Ibid.

80. Ibid. The marker on Last Stand Hill is actually a funerary marker from 1881. It has no inscription other than the names of the Seventh Cavalrymen who were killed.
81. Custer's remains are at West Point.
82. Text copied from the plaque which is in the LBNM collection.
83. Linenthal, p. 159.
84. Survey form in LBNM files.
85. Campbell is an enrolled Northern Cheyenne (Montana), but lives in Colorado.
86. "Indian Monument Bill in Limbo," 26 September, 1991; in LBNM files.
87. Published letter; in LBNM files.
88. "Congress Votes to Remove Custer Name from Battlefield," *Headquarters Heliogram;* in LBNM files.
89. U.S. Congress, Senate, Committee on Energy and Natural Resources, *Miscellaneous National Park Legislation, Hearing Before the Subcommittee on Public Lands, National Parks and Forests of the Committee on Energy and Natural Resources on H.R. 848,* 100th Cong., 1st sess., 25 July 1991, p. 63.
90. Ibid., p. 95.
91. Ibid., p. 44.
92. U.S. Congress, Senate, Select Committee on Indian Affairs, *Wounded Knee Memorial,* p. 45. This committee took testimony on both the Custer name change and the proposed Wounded Knee memorial, discussed earlier.
93. This is drawn from a copy of Utley's testimony in the LBNM files, p. 1. The testimony was presented before the Subcommittee on National Parks and Public Lands (House of Representatives) on April 23, 1991.
94. At this writing, the Indian monument authorized in that legislation is still in the planning stage.
95. Kitty Deernose interview.
96. "Indians Celebrate Renaming of Famous Site"; in LBNM files.
97. This is based on a pre-1991 estimate in Linenthal (p. 155) and a 1994 estimate made by the site staff. Indians constitute less than one percent of the nation's population so the estimate of ten percent (40,000) is quite large.

98. Gerard Baker interview, June 1994.

99. "Little Bighorn Again Inspires Passion," *The New York Times,* 23 June 1996, p. A14.

100. Ibid.

101. Public Law 101–601 [H.R. 5237], 16 November 1990. For the wide-ranging powers that NAGPRA gives Indian tribes, it is useful to consult the government's operational interpretation of that law. See Department of the Interior, "Native American Graves Protection and Repatriation Act Regulations; Proposed Rule," *Federal Register* 43, CFR, Part 10, 28 May 1993, 31122–31134. While the final rules were being hammered out, museums were required to comply with the first, and clearest, requirements of NAGPRA. These included the repatriation of all human remains and associated funerary objects. Harvard University, for example, was required to return the remains of over 10,000 individuals for reburial.

102. Barbara Isaac, "Repatriation: The New Law and the Peabody Museum," *Symbols* (A Publication of the Peabody Museum and the Department of Anthropology, Harvard University), June 1991, p. 12.

103. "The American Indian population, self-defined, has gone from 500,000 in the '60s to an estimated 2.2 million today." Mortimer B. Zuckerman, "Remember the Real Victims," *U.S. News & World Report,* 26 June 1995, p. 68. For information on the change from 1980 to 1990, see Dirk Johnson, "Census Finds Many Claiming New Identity: Indian," *New York Times,* 5 March 1991, p. A1.

2. ASIAN AMERICANS

1. Bureau of the Census data reported in Richard T. Schaefer, *Racial and Ethnic Groups,* 5th ed. (New York: Harper Collins, 1993), p. 326.

2. Asian Americans are protected as "language minorities." For more information on this term, see Abigail M. Thernstrom, *Whose Votes Count? Affirmative Action and Minority Voting Rights* (Cambridge: Harvard University Press, 1987), pp. 51–53.

3. In Yen Le Espiritu, *Asian American Panethnicity: Bridging Institutions and Identities* (Philadelphia: Temple University Press, 1992), p. 142.

4. Both men were eventually acquitted of civil rights violations as well. They served no prison time for the murder to which they had both confessed. Espiritu provides a chart (p. 147) which indicates the national ancestry of the ACJ members.

5. Espiritu, p. 134.

6. The classic sociological analyses of this phenomenon are George Simmel, *Conflict and The Web of Group-Affiliations*, trans. Kurt H. Wolff and Reinhard Bendix (Glencoe, Illinois: The Free Press, 1955), esp. pp. 96–108; and Lewis Coser, *The Functions of Social Conflict* (Glencoe, Ill.: The Free Press, 1956), esp. pp. 87–110.

7. Irene Hirano interview, May 1994.

8. See chap. 6 of Espiritu, "Reactive Solidarity: Anti-Asian Violence."

9. The standard work on Asian American history is Ronald Takaki's *Strangers from a Different Shore: A History of Asian Americans* (New York: Penguin Books, 1990). Takaki promotes the idea of a race-based Asian American identity grounded in memory of racial injustice. See especially chap. 12, "Breaking Silences: Community of Memory."

10. Espiritu, p. 17.

11. In 1970 Chinese and Japanese Americans constituted three-quarters of all Asian Americans. In 1990 they were only one-third of the population. Bureau of the Census data reported in Schaefer, p. 326.

12. Espiritu, p. 172–173.

13. Espiritu explains that "Filipino Americans have been the group most outspoken against the pan-Asian framework" (p. 104). Partly this is a function of the distinctiveness of Filipino identity. As many commentators have observed (for example, Schaefer, p. 332), the identification of Filipinos as Asian in the Census is done for geographic reasons which belie their cultural and physical differences from other Asian American groups. In this chapter I maintain the use of Filipino American in discussions of Census data, but recognize that the pan-Asian movement of the late 1960s and early 1970s was largely a Chinese and Japanese American phenomenon.

14. William Wei, *The Asian American Movement* (Philadelphia: Temple University Press, 1993), p. 22.
15. See chap. 5 of Wei, "Activists and the Development of Asian American Studies."
16. Wei, pp. 136–137.
17. Ibid.
18. Ibid., p. 47.
19. Filipinos constituted a little more than one-fifth of the Asian American population in 1970. Bureau of the Census data reported in Schaefer, p. 326.
20. Takaki, p. 488.
21. Japanese and Chinese Americans have thus far been the most active. Although less involved in the pan-Asian movement, Filipinos have also asserted their historical memories. Other groups with shorter histories in America have been less involved in the movement to reform American memory. For a general discussion of Asian American memory activism, see Wei, pp. 54–64.
22. In Richard Drinnon, *Keeper of Concentration Camps: Dillon S. Myer and American Racism* (Berkeley: University of California Press, 1987), p. 249.
23. In Drinnon, p. 153.
24. Many of those imprisoned were Japanese citizens only because U.S. law prohibited Japanese immigrants, the Issei generation, from becoming naturalized American citizens. The children of these immigrants who were born in the United States, the Nisei generation, were citizens under the Fourteenth Amendment. For a discussion of this twist in the Naturalization Law of 1870, see Roger Daniels, *Prisoners Without Trial: Japanese Americans in World War II* (New York: Hill and Wang, 1993), p. 11.
25. Daniels, p. 46.
26. In Gary Hathaway, "Tule Lake Internment Camp," 8 March 1985; in files of Eastern California Museum of Inyo County.
27. On the issue of military necessity, see the ruling of the Commission on Wartime Relocation and Internment of Citizens, *Personal Justice Denied* (Washington, D.C.: US Government Printing Office, December 1982), pp. 2–3.

28. For selections of Roosevelt's statements on racial breeding and character traits, see Christopher Thorne, *Allies of a Kind: The United States, Britain, and the War Against Japan, 1941–4* (New York: Oxford University Press, 1978), pp. 158–159, 167–168.
29. Drinnon, p. 256.
30. Full text reproduced in Daniels, pp. 129–130.
31. Ibid., p. 46.
32. In Takaki, p. 362.
33. Daniels, p. 55.
34. Eisenhower later wrote a book about his experiences with FDR. Milton S. Eisenhower, *The President Is Calling* (Garden City, New York: Doubleday, 1974). For information on the WRA period see pp. 95–127.
35. Many homes and businesses were sold for a pittance or left to a neighbor with only a verbal agreement. For more details, see the report of the Commission on Wartime Relocation and Internment of Citizens, *Personal Justice Denied,* esp. pp. 129–133.
36. The 10,000 came from Military Area No. 2, all of the eastern half of California.
37. Commission on Wartime Relocation and Internment of Civilians, p. 11.
38. In Daniels, p. 57.
39. This is an excerpt from Myer's taped autobiography. In Drinnon, p. 8.
40. The photos are reproduced in John Armor and Peter Wright, *Manzanar* (New York: Times Books, 1988). Adams's original text is inspired sarcasm.
41. Japanese Americans living in Hawaii were not detained.
42. U.S. Department of the Interior, War Relocation Authority, in collaboration with the War Department, "Nisei in Uniform," (ca. 1943), np; in files of Eastern California Museum of Inyo County. Also in Commission on Wartime Relocation and Internment of Civilians, p. 191.
43. In Drinnon, p. 163.
44. Peter Irons, *Justice at War* (Berkeley: University of California Press, 1983), p. 271. The WRA was transferred to Ickes's Department of the Interior in 1944.
45. Ibid., p. 273.
46. Armor and Wright, p. xviii.

47. In Henry Y. Ueno, *Manzanar Martyr* (Anaheim, California: Shumway Family History Services, 1986), p. v.
48. Mas Okui interview, April 1994. Okui is a retired teacher and active in Manzanar preservation.
49. William Wei describes similar efforts by Chinese Americans. He quotes one opponent of the model minority thesis as saying that the "fiction is that the Chinese have never suffered as much as, say, the black or brown communities in this country" (p. 174).
50. Although a small group of Issei (first-generation) Japanese Americans had been making pilgrimages to the site since 1946 to perform religious services for the dead, the 1969 pilgrimage was the first with an expressed political content.
51. Raymond Okamura, et al., "Campaign to Repeal the Emergency Detention Act," *Amerasia Journal* 2 (Fall 1974), p. 71. Emphasizing the connection to the Japanese experience in World War II, the text of the Detention Act is reproduced in Roger Daniels, *The Decision to Relocate the Japanese Americans* (Malabar, Fla.: Robert E. Krieger, 1986), pp. 129–130.
52. Don T. Nakanishi, "Surviving Democracy's 'Mistake': Japanese Americans & the Enduring Legacy of Executive Order 9066," *Amerasia Journal* 19 (Winter 1993), p. 16.
53. Ibid., pp. 16–18.
54. Manzanar Committee, "The Manzanar Pilgrimage: A Time for Sharing," (1981), p. 12. This is a program for the 1981 pilgrimage.
55. In Nadine Ishitani Hata, *The Historic Preservation Movement in California 1940–1976* (np: California Department of Parks and Recreation/Office of Historic Preservation, 1992), p. 170.
56. Ibid., pp. 169–170.
57. Ibid., p. 170.
58. In his book on the WRA experience, Myer explained, "Relocation centers were called 'concentration camps' by many writers and commentators, but they were very different from the normal concept of what a concentration camp is like. First of all, the centers were not prison camps." Dillon S. Myer, *Uprooted Americans: The Japanese Americans and the War Relocation Authority During World War II* (Tucson: University of Arizona Press, 1971), p. 291.

59. Ibid., p. 292.

60. Ibid., p. 286. The WRA ran a work-release program during the war which let many individuals out of the camps on the condition that they move to designated areas and take up jobs that had been lined up for them. The locations were selected for their notable lack of people of Japanese ancestry. Later, as director of the Bureau of Indian Affairs, Myer pursued a similar policy of dispersion (called "Termination") with Indian tribes. For an account of both periods of Myer's career, see Richard Drinnon's *Keeper of Concentration Camps.*

61. Eisenhower, p. 125.

62. Ibid., p. 122.

63. Manzanar Committee, "The Manzanar Pilgrimage: A Time for Sharing," p. 17.

64. In Hata, p. 170. This chronology of events is also reconstructed in Manzanar Committee, "Chronology of Events"; in files of the Manzanar Committee of Los Angeles. Copy courtesy of Sue Embry.

65. In Hata, p. 171.

66. State of California, Department of Parks and Recreation, *Manzanar: A Feasibility Study* (Sacramento: State of California, September 1974), p. 10.

67. Hata, p. 172.

68. Keith Bright interview, April 1994.

69. An earlier, though ineffectual, move toward Redress was the Japanese American Claims Act of 1948. The Act did not recognize that the internment was unjust, it simply admitted that the resulting loss of property should be compensated. Few Japanese Americans received anything under this legislation.

70. Proclamation 4417, *Federal Register,* vol. 41, no. 35 (20 February 1976). The full text of Proclamation 4417 is reprinted in Daniels, *Prisoners Without Trial,* pp. 132–133.

71. Commission on Wartime Relocation and Internment of Civilians, p. 18.

72. In Daniels, *Prisoners Without Trial,* p. 101.

73. Ibid., p. 102. H.R. 442 is numbered in honor of the 442nd Regimental Combat Team.

74. For a detailed history, see Leslie T. Hatamiya's *Righting a Wrong: Japanese Americans and the Passage of the Civil Liberties Act of 1988* (Stanford: Stanford University Press, 1993).

75. Hatamiya details the process of securing the appropriations in *Righting a Wrong*, pp. 181–190. Success breeds imitation. In 1994, Rep. John Conyers introduced legislation (H.R. 40) which called for the creation of a commission with an eight-million-dollar appropriation to explore the past injustices of slavery and their enduring economic impact. Conyers believes the report of that commission would establish cause for issuing a cash payment to all descendants of individuals brought to America in slavery. Descendants of the Indians massacred at Wounded Knee have pursued a similar goal.

76. David Lowenthal, *The Past Is Another Country* (Cambridge, England: Cambridge University Press, 1985), p. 247.

77. James M. Mayo, *War Memorials as Political Landscape: The American Experience and Beyond* (New York: Praeger, 1988), p. 216.

78. The history of the construction of that monument is related in Karal Ann Marling and John Wetenhall, *Iwo Jima: Monuments, Memories, and the American Hero* (Cambridge: Harvard University Press, 1991).

79. The Park Service proposal grew out of Public Law 95–348, which authorized the Park Service to study historic sites associated with the Pacific Campaign of World War II.

80. In Richard Potashin, "Return to Manzanar: Its Past, Its Future," *Inyo Register,* 29 April 1990; in files of Eastern California Museum of Inyo County.

81. A useful discussion of the Park Service's representation of the tragedies of American history is Robin Winks's "Sites of Shame," *National Parks: The Magazine of the National Parks and Conservation Association* 68 (March/April 1994), pp. 22–23.

82. The chronology related here is based on taped interviews with Keith Bright, Sue Embry, and Rose Ochi.

83. The simple presence of a National Park Service site can draw thousands of tourists.

84. In Momoko Murakami, "The Irony of Manzanar Relocation Center," 19 December 1990, p. 22; in files of Eastern California Museum of Inyo County.

85. The other Senator, Alan Cranston, was a supporter of the site proposal.

86. Murakami, p. 22.

87. The "stream approach" to historic site representation emphasizes the many events which occurred at a given historic site, not only that event for which the site is most famous.

88. In Manzanar Committee, "History of Manzanar," p. 2; courtesy of Sue Embry.

89. James Oda, *Heroic Struggles of Japanese Americans: Partisan Fighters from America's Concentration Camps* (np: KNI, 1981), p. i.

90. Daniels, *Prisoners Without Trial,* p. 63.

91. Gary Y. Okihiro, "Japanese Resistance in America's Concentration Camps: A Re-evaluation," *Amerasia Journal* 2 (Fall 1973), p. 32.

92. Ibid., p. 31.

93. Arthur A. Hansen and David A. Hacker, "The Manzanar Riot: An Ethnic Perspective," *Amerasia Journal* 2 (Fall 1974), p. 142.

94. Ibid.

95. James E. Young, *The Texture of Memory: Holocaust Memorials and Meaning* (New Haven: Yale University Press, 1993), p. 347.

96. Ibid.

97. Nakanishi, p. 31.

98. Mas Okui interview.

99. Chinese Americans were the other major population involved in the early pan-Asian movement. Because of recent immigration, American-born Chinese were a minority within the Chinese American population in 1990. Bureau of the Census data reported in Schaefer, p. 326.

3. LATINOS

1. People identifying themselves as "Other" within the Hispanic category make up the remaining 6.9 percent of the population. Bureau of the Census data reported in Richard T. Schaefer, *Racial and Ethnic Groups,* 5th ed. (New York: Harper Collins, 1993), p. 251.

2. Ibid., p. 252. The percentage for Mexican Americans is computed from Census data on page 256. Central Americans and others are scattered mostly in California and New York (p. 253).

3. Morris Janowitz, *The Reconstruction of Patriotism: Education for Civic Consciousness* (Chicago: University of Chicago Press, 1983), p. 137. Also in

Peter Skerry, *Mexican Americans: The Ambivalent Minority* (New York: Free Press, 1993), p. 4.

4. Schaefer, p. 266. Earl Shorris, *Latinos: A Biography of the People* (New York: W. W. Norton, 1992), pp. 62–76.

5. For a discussion of the unique character of Miami politics, see "Fulano de Cuba" in Shorris, pp. 62–76.

6. For more information on Mexican Americans and the Voting Rights Act, see Abigail M. Thernstrom, *Whose Votes Count? Affirmative Action and Minority Voting Rights* (Cambridge: Harvard University Press, 1987), pp. 43–62.

7. Shorris, p. 12.

8. A list of Latino history museums appears in Charles B. Montney, ed., and Ned Burels, assoc. ed., *Hispanic Americans Information Directory*, 3d ed. (Detroit: Gale Research, 1994), pp. 105–122. As that directory indicates, Mexican American memory activism is the most developed of all Latino ethnic groups.

9. Skerry, p. 9.

10. Ibid., p. 17.

11. Ibid.

12. Ibid., p. 9; Skerry's emphasis. The brackets here replace the term Chicano, explained later in this chapter.

13. Ibid.

14. Mario T. García, *Mexican Americans: Leadership, Ideology, & Identity, 1930–1960* (New Haven: Yale University Press, 1989), pp. 281–282. García is summarizing the arguments of Mexican American intellectual, Arthur L. Campa.

15. For a discussion of this issue, with respect to the 1980 Census, see Richard L. Nostrand's *The Hispano Homeland* (Norman: University of Oklahoma, 1992), pp. 233–237.

16. Nostrand, p. 14–15.

17. For a discussion of the relationship between economic self-interest and ethnic self-identification, see Orlando Patterson's "Context and Choice in Ethnic Allegiance: A Theoretical Framework and Caribbean Case Study," in *Ethnicity: Theory and Experience,* eds. Nathan Glazer and Daniel P. Moynihan, with the assistance of Corinne Saposs Schelling (Cambridge: Harvard University Press, 1975), pp. 305–349.

18. For a case study of this in California, see Martha K. Norkunas, *The Politics of Public Memory: Tourism, History and Ethnicity in Monterey, California* (Albany: State University of New York, 1993).

19. Observations based on site visits in 1990, 1992, and 1994.

20. For a detailed discussion of changing racial identification in Mexico, see Henry C. Schmidt, *The Roots of Lo Mexicano: Self and Society in Mexican Thought, 1900–1934* (College Station: Texas A&M University Press, 1978).

21. In Tony Castro, *Chicano Power: The Emergence of Mexican America* (New York: Saturday Review Press, 1974), p. 141. Because the use of accents in Chicano literature is quite irregular, I have standardized accented words like Joaquín and Aztlán regardless of how they appear in the original texts quoted.

22. In Stan Steiner, *La Raza: The Mexican Americans* (New York: Harper Colophon Books, 1970), p. 387.

23. Rodolfo Acuña, *Occupied America: A History of Chicanos,* 3d ed. (New York: Harper & Row, 1988), p. 338.

24. Many older Hispanics are still offended by the term.

25. Acuña, p. 336.

26. Shorris, pp. 103–4.

27. In Armando B. Rendon, *Chicano Manifesto* (New York: Macmillan, 1971), pp. 336–337. Italics in the original. There is some dispute about whether or not this was the first modern expression of the concept of Aztlán. For our purposes the precise origin is unimportant, but those interested in this subject should consult Daniel Cooper Alarcón's "The Aztec Palimpsest: Toward a New Understanding of Aztlán, Cultural Identity and History," *Aztlán* 19 (Fall 1992), pp. 33–63. For a history of the Aztlán concept in Mexican American thought before the 1960s, see John R. Chavez, *The Lost Land: The Chicano Image of the Southwest* (Albuquerque: University of New Mexico Press, 1984).

28. Rendon, p. 295.

29. Luis Valdez, "Introduction: 'La Plebe,'" in *Aztlán: An Anthology of Mexican American Literature,* eds. Luis Valdez and Stan Steiner (New York: Alfred A. Knopf, 1973), pp. xiii–xiv.

30. Skerry, p. 256.

31. Clayborne Carson, *In Struggle: SNCC and the Black Awakening of the 1960s* (Cambridge: Harvard University Press, 1981), p. 278.

32. For uses of the term "Brown Power," see Stan Steiner's *La Raza*, pp. 113–116.

33. For a detailed study of local politics in Crystal City, see John Staples Shockley, *Chicano Revolt in a Texas Town* (Notre Dame: University of Notre Dame Press, 1974).

34. In John C. Hammerback, Richard J, Jensen, and José Angel Gutiérrez, *A War of Words: Chicano Protest in the 1960s and 1970s* (Westport, Conn.: Greenwood Press, 1985), p. 96.

35. See, for example, Henry Gonzáles's "Reverse Racism," in *Aztlán: An Anthology,* pp. 311–318.

36. Skerry, p. 264.

37. Mario Barrera, *Beyond Aztlán: Ethnic Autonomy in Comparative Perspective* (New York: Praeger, 1988), p. 44.

38. In Jack Forbes, *Aztecas del Norte: The Chicanos of Aztlán* (Greenwich, Conn.: Fawcett, 1973), p. 175.

39. Even there its future seems uncertain. See my discussion of articles in the journal *Aztlán* below.

40. Shorris, p. 100.

41. Alarcón, p. 39. *Aztlán* itself is a product of Chicano radicalism of the early 1970s.

42. Rosa Linda Fregoso and Angie Chabram, "Chicana/o Cultural Representation: Reframing Alternative Critical Discourses," *Cultural Studies* 4 (October 1990), p. 206.

43. The efforts of black Afrocentrists to promote a constructed past have been considerably more successful. See Chapter 4.

44. García, p. 300.

45. Juan Bruce-Novoa, "History as Content, History as Act: The Chicano Novel," *Aztlán* 18 (Spring 1989), p. 42.

46. Paul Andrew Hutton, introduction to Susan Prendergast Schoelwer with Tom W. Glaser, *Alamo Images: Changing Perceptions of a Texas Experience* (Dallas: DeGolyer Library and Southern Methodist University Press, 1985), p. 6.

47. For a discussion of this period's fascination with history, see Part Two of Michael Kammen's *Mystic Chords of Memory: The Transformation of Tradition in American Culture* (New York: Alfred A. Knopf, 1991).

48. For more information on the DRT, see the chapter "Matronly Daughters" in Holly Beachley Brear, *Inherit the Alamo: Myth and Ritual at an American Shrine* (Austin: University of Texas Press, 1995).

49. Brear, p. 84.

50. For a detailed history of these organizations, see ibid. Brear reports on the membership of the Cavaliers on page 110.

51. Her full title is "Queen of the Order of the Alamo." Ibid., p. 19.

52. Before 1913 the festival was known as the Battle of the Flowers. Ibid., p. 13.

53. Rey Feo is "a Fiesta personality based on the medieval Ugly King crowned by peasants of southern Europe to mock their established royalty." Ibid., pp. 21–22.

54. This assertion is based on a review of the "Protests" file which the DRT keeps in their archive at the Alamo. The only recorded protest action within the DRT's compound was a trivial incident involving three self-proclaimed Maoists who scaled the walls in 1980. A protest that occurred in 1988, described below, was outside the walls.

55. For a discussion of these difference see Skerry, passim.

56. Bureau of the Census data reported in Skerry, p. 61.

57. Skerry provides a statistical comparison of the political representation of Hispanics in Los Angeles and San Antonio city politics (p. 105–106).

58. Ibid., p. 39.

59. Gilberto Hinojosa interview, March 1995.

60. Ibid.

61. Robert Benavides interview, March 1995.

62. Gary Gabehart interview, March 1995.

63. Ibid.

64. For a discussion of this change see Schmidt, *The Roots of Lo Mexicano,* passim.

65. For a discussion of the flag issue see Albert A. Nofi, *The Alamo and the Texas War of Independence* (New York: Da Capo Press, 1994), p. 129.

66. Flyer in files of the Daughters of the Republic of Texas.

67. Gilberto Hinojosa interview. Holly Brear also describes the IMAX protest, pp. 115–116, 119–120.

68. Robert Benavides interview.

69. Gilberto Hinojosa interview.

70. Hector D. Cantu, "LULAC Surrenders Alamo Bid," *San Antonio Light,* 15 May 1988, pp. B1, B4.

71. In J. Michael Parker and Stefanie Scott, "DRT Gears Up for Another Fight with State Over Alamo," *San Antonio Express-News,* 2 March 1993; in the files of the Daughters of the Republic of Texas. Wilson resubmitted his proposal in 1993 and 1995.

72. Jim Hutton, "Indian Group's Entry on Scene a Surprise," *San Antonio Express-News,* 20 February 1994, pp. 1A, 8A.

73. Marty Sabota, "Alamo Burial-Record Finding Sprang from Search for Roots," *San Antonio Express-News,* 26 January 1994, p. A8.

74. In Brear, p. 113.

75. Sabota, p. A8.

76. Cover sheet summary of the Alamo Plaza Study Committee's *Report and Recommendations to City Council* (San Antonio: np, 20 October 1994).

77. Howard Peak interview, March 1995.

78. Alamo Plaza Study Committee, *Report,* p. 7.

79. Gilberto Hinojosa interview.

80. Robert Benavides interview.

81. Gary Gabehart interview.

82. Similar ambivalence exists among Filipinos, who can choose to identify with pan-Asian or Latino movements in America. See Yen Le Espiritu, *Asian American Pan-ethnicity: Bridging Institutions and Identities* (Philadelphia: Temple University Press, 1992), passim.

4. BLACKS

1. For an overview of the development of American collective memory since 1870, see Michael Kammen, *Mystic Chords of Memory: The Transformation of Tradition in American Culture* (New York: Alfred A. Knopf, 1991).

2. See in particular C. Vann Woodward's essay, "A Southern Critique for the Gilded Age," in *The Burden of Southern History* (Baton Rouge: Louisiana State University Press, 1960).

3. In David W. Blight, *Frederick Douglass' Civil War: Keeping Faith in Jubilee* (Baton Rouge: Louisiana State University Press, 1989), p. 219. The chapter "Douglass and the Struggle for the Memory of the Civil War" outlines Douglass' thought on the importance of collective memory.

4. Ibid., p. 224.

5. There is a growing literature on alternative collective memory celebrations among blacks. See, for example, William H. Wiggins, Jr., *O Freedom!: Afro-American Emancipation Celebrations* (Knoxville: The University of Tennessee Press, 1987).

6. A vivid account of the physical and cultural separation that occurred during that time is Joel Williamson's *The Crucible of Race: Black-White Relations in the American South Since Emancipation* (New York: Oxford University Press, 1984).

7. In Williamson, p. 176. President Wilson made his own contribution to the pro-South interpretation of the Civil War in *Robert E. Lee, an Interpretation* (Chapel Hill: The University of North Carolina Press, 1924).

8. W. J. Cash, *The Mind of the South* (New York: Alfred A. Knopf, Inc., 1941), pp. 49–50.

9. In Blight, p. 223.

10. In Wiggins, p. 45. For a history of the development of Negro History Week and Black History Month, see Alfred Young, "The Historical Origin and Significance of the Afro-American History Month Observance," *Negro History Bulletin* 45 (Oct./Nov./Dec. 1982), pp. 100–101.

11. A short history of the black museum industry appears later in this chapter.

12. Often the slaves themselves were overlooked altogether. For a brief history of the restoration and interpretation of Colonial Williamsburg, see Kammen, pp. 359–370, 581–587. Debate about the interpretation of black history there continues. See, for example, Eric Gable et al., "On the Uses of Relativism: Fact, Conjecture, and Black and White Histories at Colonial Williamsburg," *American Ethnologist* 19 (November 1992), pp. 791–805.

13. W. E. Burghardt Du Bois, *Black Reconstruction: An Essay Toward a History of the Part Which Black Folk Played in the Attempt to Reconstruct Democracy in America, 1860–1880* (New York: Harcourt, Brace, 1935), pp. 731, 733. For an account of the professionalization of black history, see August Meier and Elliott Rudwick, *Black History and the Historical Profession, 1915–1980* (Urbana: University of Illinois Press, 1986).

14. Ibid., p. 714.

15. Ibid., p. 728.

16. Ibid., p. 711.

17. Ibid., p. 723.

18. Ibid., p. 711.

19. W. E. B. Du Bois, *The Souls of Black Folk* (New York: Alfred A Knopf, 1993), pp. 8–9.

20. Richard Wright, *12 Million Black Voices,* in *Richard Wright Reader,* eds. Ellen Wright and Michel Fabre (New York: Harper & Row, 1978), p. 240.

21. James Baldwin, *The Fire Next Time,* in *The Price of the Ticket: Collected Nonfiction, 1948–1985* (New York: St. Martin's, 1985), p. 335.

22. Ibid., p. 336.

23. Ibid., p. 378.

24. Malcolm X, *Malcolm X on Afro-American History,* expanded and illustrated ed. (New York: Pathfinder Press, 1970), p. 55.

25. Martin Luther King, Jr., *Where Do We Go from Here? Chaos or Community* (New York: Harper & Row, 1967), p. 41.

26. Arthur A. Schomburg, "The Negro Digs Up His Past," in *Anthology of American Negro Literature,* ed. Sylvestre C. Watkins (New York: The Modern Library, 1944), p. 101.

27. Du Bois, *Black Reconstruction,* p. 727.

28. Martin Luther King, Jr., "The Ethical Demands for Integration," in *A Testament of Hope: The Essential Writing of Martin Luther King, Jr.,* ed. James M. Washington (San Francisco: Harper & Row, 1986), p. 124.

29. Although Ricks and Carmichael did not author "Black Power," it was their actions in Mississippi which forever associated that slogan with cul-

tural radicalism. See Clayborne Carson, *In Struggle: SNCC and the Black Awakening of the 1960s* (Cambridge: Harvard University Press, 1981), p. 209.

30. Robert Penn Warren, *Who Speaks for the Negro?* (New York: Random House, 1965), p. 396. I have omitted a redundant exchange within this interview which appears between Warren's first question and Carmichael's first response.

31. Stokely Carmichael and Charles V. Hamilton, *Black Power: The Politics of Liberation in America* (New York: Random House, 1967), pp. 34–35.

32. Orlando Patterson, "Rethinking Black History," *Harvard Educational Review* 4 (August 1971), pp. 297–298.

33. I say "modern" because Afrocentrism has a tradition, often not well understood, that goes back generations before Garvey. See Wilson Jeremiah Moses, *Black Messiahs and Uncle Toms: Social and Literary Manipulations of a Religious Myth,* rev. ed. (University Park: Pennsylvania State University Press, 1993).

34. In Mary Lefkowitz, "Not Out of Africa: The Origins of Greece and the Illusions of Afrocentrists," *The New Republic,* 210 (10 February 1992), p. 31.

35. Marcus Garvey, *Marcus Garvey: Life and Lessons, A Centennial Companion to the Marcus Garvey and Universal Negro Improvement Association Papers,* ed. Robert A. Hill and assoc. ed. Barbara Bair (Berkeley: University of California Press, 1987), p. 293.

36. Ibid.

37. Ibid., pp. 290, 293.

38. Ibid., pp. 193–194.

39. Malcolm X, *Malcolm X on Afro-American History,* p. 3.

40. Ibid., pp. 55–56.

41. Ibid., p. 74.

42. Herbert J. Gans, "Comment: Ethnic Invention and Acculturation, A Bumpy Line Approach," *Journal of American Ethnic History* 12 (Fall 1992), p. 43.

43. Maulana Karenga, *The African American Holiday of Kwanzaa* (Los Angeles: University of Sankore Press, 1988), p. 34.

44. Maulana Karenga, *The Quotable Karenga,* in Floyd B. Barbour, ed., *The Black Power Revolt: A Collection of Essays* (Boston: Extending Horizons Books, 1968), p. 162.

45. Ibid., p. 166.

46. Karenga, *The African American Holiday of Kwanzaa,* p. 30. Emphasis in original deleted.

47. Ibid., p. 54.

48. Ibid., p. 64.

49. Molefi Kete Asante, *Kemet, Afrocentricity and Knowledge* (Philadelphia: Temple University Press, 1987), p. 10.

50. Molefi Kete Asante, *Afrocentricity,* new rev. ed. (Trenton, New Jersey: African World Press, 1988), p. 25.

51. Ibid., p. 21.

52. In Warren, p. 216.

53. Henry Louis Gates, Jr., "Beware of the New Pharaohs," *Newsweek,* 23 September 1991, p. 47.

54. Karenga, *The African American Holiday of Kwanzaa,* p. 55.

55. Clarence E. Walker, "You Can't Go Home Again: The Problem of Afrocentrism," *Prospects* 18 (1993), pp. 535–536.

56. Ibid., p. 542.

57. Michael Eric Dyson, *Making Malcolm: The Myth & Meaning of Malcolm X* (New York: Oxford University Press, 1995), pp. 109–110.

58. Ibid., p. 98.

59. Walker, p. 542.

60. This was a comment by a student in my Boston Area Studies course at Harvard.

61. Patterson, p. 315.

62. While they are not numerous, Afrocentric museums exist. They range from the spacious California Afro-American Museum in Los Angeles (1977) to the tiny APEX in Atlanta (1978). For a list, see the African American Museums Association's *Blacks in Museums: A Directory of African American Museums and Museum Professionals* (Wilberforce, Ohio: African American Museums Association, 1993–94).

63. This statement is based on reported founding dates for members of the African American Museums Association. There may have been black

history museums before the Civil Rights Movement which failed to survive and thus are not represented in this count. James Oliver Horton
and Spencer R. Crew grapple with the problem of documenting earlier
museums in "Afro-Americans and Museums: Towards a Policy of Inclusion," in *History Museums in the United States: A Critical Assessment,* eds.
Warren Leon and Roy Rosenzweig (Urbana: University of Illinois Press,
1989).

64. State of Illinois, *Illinois Generations: A Traveler's Guide to African American
Heritage* (Chicago: Performance Media, nd), p. 21.

65. This information is taken from the 1989 and 1993–94 editions of the
African American Museums Association's *Blacks in Museums.* This is a directory of member museums only. Doubtless, more museums exist.

66. Christopher Columbus, an Italian, is the only other historical person
whom the states and national government so honor.

67. The Martin Luther King, Jr. Federal Holiday Commission, "The Martin
Luther King, Jr. Federal Holiday: History of Major Legislative Events"
(Atlanta: nd), np.

68. For an analysis of the role of race in the 1968 election, see Thomas
Burne Edsall and Mary D. Edsall, *Chain Reaction: The Impact of Race,
Rights, and Taxes on American Politics* (New York: W.W. Norton, 1992).

69. Kenneth O'Reilly, following Gary Wills, describes Agnew as "Nixon's
Nixon—a baiter of blacks and kids." Kenneth O'Reilly, *"Racial Matters":
The FBI's Secret File on Black America, 1960–1972* (New York: The Free
Press, 1989), p. 329.

70. A full discussion of Hoover's attempts to discredit King is in O'Reilly,
ibid., and in David Garrow, *The FBI and Martin Luther King, Jr.: From
"Solo" to Memphis* (New York: W.W. Norton, 1981).

71. This document was declassified in 1978 as a result of David Garrow's
investigative work. The memo was subsequently included in a collection
of "Additional Material Submitted for the Record" during the hearings
on S.2630, the bill to establish King's home as a national historic site.
Congressional Record, 11 September 1980, p. 156.

72. O'Reilly, p. 332.

73. Ibid., p. 332.

74. Ibid., p. 355.

75. Ibid., p. 332.

76. David J. Garrow, "The Helms Attack On King," *Southern Exposure* 12 (March/April 1984), p. 13.

77. Ibid., pp. 13, 15.

78. The Martin Luther King, Jr. Federal Holiday Commission, "The Martin Luther King, Jr. Federal Holiday: History of Major Legislative Events," np. Some states combined King's birthday with other celebrations. South Carolina, for example, combined the King observance with that of Robert E. Lee.

79. Ibid.

80. Ibid.

81. Garrow, "The Helms Attack on King," p. 12.

82. New Hampshire has a Civil Rights holiday but does not specifically recognize King. New Hampshire's continuing opposition to the King holiday is discussed in Arnie Alpert's *Stride Toward King Day* (Concord, New Hampshire: American Friends Service Committee, 1992).

83. In ibid., p. 12. For more on Thurmond and the holiday, see Nadine Cohodas, *Strom Thurmond & the Politics of Southern Change* (New York: Simon & Schuster, 1993), p. 481–484.

84. Visitation figures for many museums are reported in the American Association of Museums, *The Official Museum Directory,* 25th anniv. ed. (New Providence, NJ: R. R. Bowker, 1994). King received 766,000 visitors in 1993; Kennedy 20,000; Lincoln 292,000; Washington, 160,000. All sites are run by the National Park Service.

85. Dean Rowley interview, January 1994.

86. During much of 1993–95, I interviewed Park Service rangers around the country about their work. These observations are based on scores of such conversations.

87. Gayle Hazelwood, speech to the Chiefs of Interpretation, Lowell, MA, March 1993. Author in attendance.

88. Dean Rowley interview.

89. Stephen B. Oates, *Let the Trumpet Sound: The Life of Martin Luther King, Jr.* (New York: Harper & Row, 1982), p. 462.

90. King, "A Time to Break Silence," p. 241.

91. King, *Where Do We Go From Here,* p. 131–132.

92. Oates, pp. 387–462.

93. Dean Rowley interview.

94. In David J. Garrow, *Bearing the Cross: Martin Luther King, Jr., and the Southern Christian Leadership Conference* (New York: William Morrow, 1986), p. 625.

INDEX

Abernathy, Ralph, 114, 115
Adams, Ansel, 49, 50
African Americans. *See* Blacks
Afrocentrism: defined, 104; propo-
   nents of, 105–109; critiques of,
   109–111; and Americanist black
   history, 122–123; museums, 154
   n.62
Agnew, Spiro, 12, 114
Alamo, 6, 80–93; Order of the, 82;
   and San Antonio Cavaliers, 82;
   and King Antonio, 82–83; and
   Rey Feo, 82–83, 84; IMAX film
   on, 87–89; Plaza Study Commit-
   tee, 91–92; protest at, 149 n.54.
   See also San Antonio
Alcatraz, 11–12
American Citizens for Justice (ACJ),
   39
American Indian Movement (AIM),
   4, 12–14, 21–22, 24, 28–29
American Indians, 4, 6, 8–37, 86,
   125–126; reservation, 11–12, 15,
   37; urban, 10–12, 15, 36–37, 86
Americanist black history: defined,
   104; celebration of, 111–113; and
   Afrocentrism, 122–123. *See also*
   Black history museums; King,
   Martin Luther: National Historic
   Site
Angelou, Maya, 1–2, 8–9

Asante, Molefi Kete, 108, 109. *See
   also* Afrocentrism
Asian Americans, 4, 6, 7, 38–66, 67,
   68, 69, 93, 125–126
Aztlán, 74–75, 77–79

Baker, Gerard, 34–35
Baldwin, James, 100–101
Benavides, Robert, 85–86, 87, 88, 92
Birmingham Civil Rights Museum. *See*
   Black history museums
Black history museums: lack of,
   97–98; creation of, 112–113;
   Birmingham Civil Rights Museum,
   113, 119, 122, 123; Memphis
   Civil Rights Museum, 113, 119,
   122, 123; Martin Luther King, Jr.
   National Historic Site, 117–123
Black Power, 3–4, 10, 42, 73, 75,
   94, 102–104
Blacks, 4, 6, 7, 94–123, 125–126
Booher, Barbara, 30, 33–34
Bright, Keith, 56, 61
Brown Power, 75
Brown, Dee, 17
Bureau of Indian Affairs (BIA), 12, 13
Bush, George, 58, 62

Campaign for Redress, 56–58
Campbell, Ben Nighthorse, 31, 32
Caravan of Broken Treaties, 12, 20